Good Books Good Friends Good Food

A SUCCESSFUL RECIPE
FOR YOUR OWN BOOK CLUB

Elizabeth Weiler and Karisa Creer

Layout and Design by Kerry Hutchins

Special thanks to:

Todd Weiler

Rachel Garcia

Jyl Pattee

Spencer Hutchins

© Good Books Good Friends, L.L.C. 2002
1248 West 1900 South
Woods Cross, Utah 84087
(801) 294-4811

ISBN 0-9726189-152995

Dedicated to our Book Club

left to right: standing, Christine King, Lori Poole, Mindy Shaw,
seated, Kiersten Creer, Elizabeth Weiler, Karisa Creer, Launee Fowler

Thank you for your years of friendship and support, and all of your
very important contributions to this book!

Table of Contents

JANUARY
RESOLUTIONS / INTROSPECTION

Tuesdays with Morrie by Mitch Albom–Marshmallow Brownies
Standing for Something by Gordon B. Hinckley–Chocolate Cherry Stack-ups
The Screwtape Letters by C.S. Lewis–Lemon Squares
The Color of Water by James McBride–Seven Layer Bars

FEBRUARY
LOVE STORIES

Pride and Prejudice by Jane Austin–Pecan Cups with Raspberry Cheesecake Filling
The Scarlet Pimpernel by Baroness Emmuska Orczy–Red Velvet Cake
Jane Eyre by Charlotte Bronte–Black Forest Cake
The Princess Bride by William Goldman–Heavenly Cheesecake

MARCH
MYSTERY MONTH

Sherlock Holmes by Sir Arthur Conan Doyle–Sting of the Bee Cake
Rebecca by Daphne DuMaurier–Ice Cream Cake Roll
Great Expectations by Charles Dickens–Death by Chocolate Cake
Drowning Ruth by Christina Schwarz–Coconut Cream Cake

APRIL
TEA PARTY MONTH

Cold Sassy Tree by Olive Ann Burns–Cherry Delights
A Tale of Two Cities by Charles Dickens–Sun-Dried Tomato and Basil Butter
Mansfield Park by Jane Austen–Cucumber Sandwiches
A Tree Grows in Brooklyn by Betty Smith–Miniature Tarts

MAY
ADVENTURE MONTH

The Three Musketeers by Alexandre Dumas–Strawberry Spinach Salad
Robinson Crusoe by Daniel Defoe–Strawberry Shortcake
Island of the Blue Dolphins by Scott O'Dell–Strawberry Fruit Smoothie
The Eagle has Landed by Jack Higgins–Strawberry Pretzel Dessert

JUNE & JULY
Long Summer Books

The Brothers Karamazov by Fyodor Dostoyevsky–Veggie Pizza
Les Miserables by Victor Hugo–Shrimp Cocktail Dip
Don Quixote by Miguel de Cervantes–Taco Bean Dip
Vanity Fair by William Makepeace Thackeray–Chocolate Chip Cheeseball

AUGUST
Vacation Books

The Poisonwood Bible by Barbara Kingsolver–Chips and Fresh Salsas
All Creatures Great and Small by James Herriot –Frozen Fruit Cocktail
The Divine Secrets of the Ya-Ya Sisterhood by Rebecca Wells–Chocolate Cream Pie
Charms for the Easy Life by Kaye Gibbons–Fresh Peach Dessert

SEPTEMBER
Kid's Favorites

Harry Potter and the Sorcerer's Stone by J.K. Rowlings–Peanut Butter Rice Crispies
The Chronicles of Narnia by C.S. Lewis–Miniature Banana Muffins
Anne of Green Gables by L.M. Montgomery–Jell-O Pudding Poke Cake
To Kill a Mockingbird by Harper Lee–Spudnuts

OCTOBER
Scary Books

Dracula by Bram Stoker–Caramel Apple Dip
Frankenstein by Mary Shelley–Nutty Marshmallow Popcorn
The Strange Case of Dr. Jekyll and Mr. Hyde by Robert Louis Stevenson–Orange Bow Knots
The Phantom of the Opera by Gaston Leroux–Cinnamon Rolls

NOVEMBER
International Classics

Things Fall Apart by Chinua Achebe–Frosty Pumpkin Dessert
The Hunchback of Notre Dame by Victor Hugo–Pumpkin Roll
The Red Badge of Courage by Stephen Crane–Marbled Pumpkin Cheesecake
David Copperfield by Charles Dickens–Apple Pie

DECEMBER
Christmas Books

A Christmas Carol and Christmas Books by Charles Dickens–English Toffee
Tending Roses by Lisa Wingate–Chocolate Trifle
Little Women by Louisa May Alcott–Peanut Butter Kiss Cookies
The Giver by Lois Lowry–Chocolate Covered Caramel Pretzels

GOOD BOOKS, GOOD FRIENDS, GOOD FOOD

A Successful Recipe For Your Own Book Club
By
Elizabeth Weiler and Karisa Creer

Layout and Design by Kerry Hutchins

PREFACE

We met on the third Wednesday of January 2002, at 7:30 p.m., the same time of the month that we always met, yet this night was a little more special than usual. Not only was it our first time meeting in Lori's brand new house, but Kiersten was also there with her three week old baby, Davis. These were two very exciting events for us! That night marked our fourth anniversary as a book club. "Where had the time gone?" we asked. The years that had passed were filled with wonderful memories and close friendships. When our group came together, we had relationships on so many different levels: mother and daughter, sisters-in-law, neighbors and strangers. After four years together, we had grown very close to one another.

We tried to remember all of the books we had read together, 48 in all. "Remember 'The Scarlet Pimpernel?' It was one of the first books we read, and still one of my favorites," someone commented. Other members mentioned their favorites, and even a few that they did not care for (none of which are included in this book.) Of course, the conversation eventually turned to food. As women we hate to admit it, but we love food! Get a room full of friends together and some good food, and you have a party. Everyone reminds Christine that we need her Heavenly Cheesecake recipe, and Elizabeth's Pumpkin Roll recipe. Karisa has the great idea that we should combine our recipes into a book. Then she takes her idea a step further and says, "What we should do is write a book club book. We could include all the great books we have read and all the recipes. We could write a book that Oprah would be proud of!"

Then, of course, we wondered if we really could write a book, and if we did, whether Oprah would have us on her show. It was all fun and games after that, except for the sleepless nights when all the ideas were flowing through our heads, and we were so excited that we could not sleep. We could not believe that a book like this had not been written already. Book Clubs are all the rage, so we get a lot of questions about how we run ours. Soon the whole incentive for writing the book was to give others the encouragement to start their own Book Club.

The hardest thing for our book club is finding a day that we can all meet. We are all stay-at-home mothers, except for Launee, who is Karisa's mother, because her children are grown. So when you start juggling all of our busy family schedules, it is a task to say the least. We have changed our nights a couple of times during the four years to accommodate members' schedules. Usually we try to pick a certain night of the month and stick with it. We begin at 7:30 p.m., which gives our husbands time to get home from work, and us time to have dinner with our families. Once dinner is over we head out the door, crossing our fingers and hoping that our husbands will have the kids in bed, asleep, by the time we get home.

We plan our meetings at least six months in advance, allowing everyone to choose the book and recipe their respective month. So at each January meeting, the hostess of the February meeting will announce the next month's book. This process is followed each subsequent month. The hostess is in charge of the book discussion, and should have prepared some questions to ask the group. She should also present some interesting facts about the author. Book club members bring their own copy of the book, and should share with the group the part (or parts) of the book that really moved them.

During some meetings we could go on and on about the book, while during others there was not as much to discuss. It is enlightening to hear other member's perspectives. Sometimes a comment is made, and it's one of those "aha" moments, when the light bulb turns on, and you see things in a different way. You'll often hear one of us say, "I would have never thought of that before, you're right." or "Yes, but what about . . . ." Once we've finished with the book, we've only just begun. We always have lots of other things to talk about, as we enjoy our dessert.

Our book club holds two parties a year, both of which are a big hit. As you review the table of contents, you will see that we have combined the months of June and July together. As such, June's hostess has the chance to choose a big, long book. For instance, Les Miserables is more than 1,400 pages, and although we all LOVE to read, 1,400 pages is more material than our group of busy ladies can get through in a month. Our first party comes into play in July. The July hostess does not choose a book, but rather plans our annual family barbecue. She can have it at her home, or at a park, and is also in charge of making the food assignments. The picnic is a great time for our families to be together, and it is always fun to watch the kids play. Some of our children are cousins, and others will see each other only once a year. Since all of our children are under the age of nine, they are still very accepting of each other, and have a blast together. It is always fun to see the husbands get together and talk about "manly stuff", like football. During our July picnic, we usually ask each other, "How is the book coming?" or "How far have you gotten?" but we don't discuss the substance of the book until August.

We also have a Christmas Party each December. Unlike our summer picnic, our Christmas party is for book club members only. The member in charge can plan whatever she wants. We have had a nice sit-down Christmas dinner before and we have also been served a dessert only. But the one tradition we follow each December is our book exchange. Everyone brings a new gift-wrapped book. We choose numbers out of a hat and the person with the lowest number gets to choose and open the first book. The person with the second lowest number then either steals the first member's book, or selects a different one. If you have your book taken, you get to choose another book to unwrap, or steal someone else's book. A single book can only be stolen three times. The third person to steal a book gets to take it home. You may have played this game before - it is a derivative of the popular white elephant gift exchange. It is a lot of fun.

Last year, we also had a tea party. Elizabeth was the hostess, and with some help from her English friend, Kerry, she tried to make it as authentic as possible. The tea party went so well that it will become an annual event. The principle is that you should be creative and have fun with your club! Book club is not just about the books we read, it's about the time we spend together as friends, the much needed breaks we take from our homes and families, and the opportunity for some good old fashioned "girl talk". You'll soon find that nothing comes between you and your favorite night out as you politely refuse other requests explaining, "I'm sorry, but that's my book club night."

We have designed this book with four recipes and four book suggestions for each month. We have also grouped them into categories where possible. We hope that this book will give you some good ideas and a little incentive to start your own book club! It has been an amazing adventure for us and we are grateful to Kiersten who took the initiative and started ours. Quoting from the book, **Standing for Something**, "No matter how old we become, we can acquire knowledge and use it. We can gather wisdom and profit from it. We can grow and progress and improve - and, in the process, strengthen the lives of those within our circle of influence." Take time for yourself and improve your mind. Let your children see you enjoying books, and enjoy books together with your children. September's selections are designated as 'kid's favorites", so you may be able to enjoy them together. Remember, "you will reap what you sow", so when choosing a book, choose wisely, and fill your mind with good, uplifting things.

The only thing left to do is to thumb through the pages of this beautiful book, find a book that intrigues you, and start reading!

GETTING STARTED

Determining Who to Invite.

This is the first and most important step! The people that you choose to join your book club will become a big part of your life, and will hopefully become some of your best friends. Choose people whom you know to be dependable. Your book club will not be successful if the members pick and choose the meetings they want to attend. All of your members should be excited and willing to make book club a priority. They should be dedicated to attending each meeting after reading that month's selection. Also, make sure to select people who will enjoy reading and will "make time" to complete the books each month. It takes a certain amount of commitment to complete a book each month. Most people are already busy with a full schedule. Be sure to select people who will get up a little earlier, or take some time during a child's nap, or read in bed before falling asleep.

Like most good things in life, book club requires some sacrifice, but is a very enriching investment of time. Something else to consider is whether any one person would tend to dominate your book club conversation. Try to choose people who will enjoy hearing everyone's opinion. If you are planning to ask your members to take turns hosting, consider whether each person would enjoy taking a turn holding book club at their home and providing refreshments for the group.

In considering how many members to invite, one obvious factor is how many people you can accommodate in your home. If you end up with a large group, some members may not be able to host a meeting. It is important for everyone to be comfortable and cozy. How many people do you consider a good group for conversation? We have found that a group of approximately seven is good for us and our circumstances. You will want everyone to be included the conversation, and have an opportunity to share their insights. You may find that a smaller or larger group works better for you. You may also want to consider the fact that occasionally someone will have to miss, and you will still want to have enough people to feel like a group and have an interesting conversation.

Holding a Planning Meeting.

After you have made your list of members, and decided who and how many to invite, you are ready to send out invitations. You will then be prepared for your first meeting. There are several things that you will need to decide as a group at this meeting. First, what type of book is the group interested in reading: modern, classic, religious, romance, etc. The list could go on and on. How does your group feel about books with profanity and sexual content? You may want to discuss the type of subject matter that everyone will be comfortable reading. Be very specific; it is not going to be enjoyable and worth everyone's time to read the book if it is not interesting to them or if the content is offensive to some people. And if some members do not read the book, they will not feel a great desire to come to book club.

Next, how often do you want to meet? Our book club meets once per month on the fourth Thursday, but you could meet more or less often, depending on your preferences. Some groups may want to meet quarterly. What time do you want to meet? Our group meets at 7:30 p.m. on weekday evenings, which gives us time to have dinner with our families, but our discussions will often go past 10:00 p.m. Since all of the members of our group are married with children, our husbands are left with the responsibility of getting the kids to bed. You may choose to meet earlier in the day, on a weekend evening, or even on a weekend morning or afternoon. The important thing is that you choose a day and time and stick with it. That way your members can have it on the calendar, and plan their schedules around it.

Will your group rotate to every member's home, meet at the same person's home each time, or make reservations at a restaurant, a library, church, or community center? The location you choose will have a huge impact on your book club. Our book club experience has been defined by rotating through our members' homes. We make up a schedule several months in advance so that each member can choose a month that works best for her. Our experience would have been drastically different if we had elected to meet at a local library. There are many options, so be creative.

Will your club allow members to bring small children? This was an important issue to our book club as we all have young and growing families. When our book club started, we collectively had thirteen children. Within four years we have experienced the birth of ten more children, with another two due in 2003! We voted to not allow children at our meetings, with the exception of nursing babies. If you choose to bring your children, you may want to consider meeting at a park, and perhaps hire a sitter so that the mothers are not constantly being distracted. We have had nights when schedules unexpectedly change, and either someone had to bring a child or not come at all. The hostess and mother should make that decision together. Perhaps that child could come and quietly watch a video in another room.

As much as we've stressed consistence, we also know that it is important to be flexible. Schedules change, people move, priorities get shuffled, etc. Find a new day or time that works for everyone, and then try to stick with it as long as possible. If someone moves, or is unable to continue as a member of your book club, then you may need to decide as a group if you will fill the vacancy. If you do elect to replace a departing member, then it is important to find someone who will fit in with the rest of your group. In any event, be willing to be flexible.

Understanding your Responsibilities as a Hostess.

As the hostess, you should announce your book selection at least one month in advance. Our club always announces the next month's book at our monthly meetings. Choosing a book can sometimes be difficult. If you have no idea of what title to choose, you should ask friends and family members for recommendations. You could also ask someone at the library or your favorite book store. Go on-line and check out other book club lists (i.e., Oprah, Regis and Kelly, Good Morning America, The Today Show).

Once the hostess has selected and announced her book selection choice in a timely manner, she should mail each member a reminder before the meeting. We have some avid "scrap bookers" in our group and they have sent out some very cute reminder postcards. Although mailed reminders are strongly recommended, a good hostess will also place a follow up telephone call to each member a week before the meeting.

We start our discussion by giving a little background on the author and/or book. Some of our authors have lived incredible lives; you will find this part of the meeting very interesting. You may even be surprised and find that someone you thought of as a male author, is really female, and vice versa. It's also fun to hear about other things that were going on in the world when the book was written, that may have influenced the author. This information can be found on book jackets, or acknowledgments written by the author in the book. The internet is also a wonderful source, as well as the library and autobiographies written about the author. We hope that you'll enjoy the interesting facts we have included in this book about some of our favorite authors.

It is also fun to prepare one or two discussion questions and/or mark a favorite part of the story to share with the group, to get the discussion flowing. You may use the discussion questions that we've included in this book, or make up your own. We have tried to include basic discussion "sparkers" that do not give away any major plot lines. We have never had a lull in conversation in our group, and doubt that any other group of women would - it's not our nature. Our problem is bringing the meeting to an end; we've had some pretty long nights in the past. Once you've finished discussing the book, you'll find plenty more to talk about, and that's an important part of book club. This is a much deserved time to be away from family, work and life's stresses. Relax, and enjoy yourself!

Of course, what's a party without food! This is the part we all look forward to the most. As the hostess, you get to prepare one of your favorite recipes (unless you are at a restaurant.) We usually serve desserts, or finger foods, but we have on special occasions had a complete dinner, or a tea party. Finger foods work best if you are meeting around a table. If you are meeting in a living or family room, you may want to prepare something that you can serve individually to each person. Be creative and have fun with food. That is how this book began; we all wanted each others recipes, and it bloomed from there. We have included all the recipes we have served over the past four years; they range from incredibly simple to the gourmet, so we hope that there will be something for everyone.

Being the hostess is a lot of fun. It takes some preparation, but is very rewarding. When your turn is over, it is nice to know that for the next few months you just relax and enjoy yourself.

*"The love of learning,
the sequestered nooks,
and all the sweet
serenity of books."*
       Longfellow

January

RESOLUTIONS AND INTROSPECTION

Many people have come to view January as a month of contemplation. With January being the start of a new year, a new beginning, it seems the perfect time to look within ourselves and resolve the way we have been living with the way we hope to live in the future. It gives us an opportunity to reflect and turn our focus back to what really matters in life. The book selections featured for January were chosen with these thoughts in mind. All of them, in one way or another, have helped us to look at life with renewed appreciation, greater perspective and heightened enthusiasm for self-improvement.

TUESDAYS WITH MORRIE
by
Mitch Albom

"The last class of my old professor's life took place once a week in his house, by a window in the study where he could watch a small hibiscus plant shed its pink leaves. The class met on Tuesdays. It began after breakfast. The subject was The Meaning of Life. It was taught from experience.

No grades were given, but there were oral exams each week. You were expected to respond to questions, and you were expected to pose questions of your own. You were also required to perform physical tasks now and then, such as lifting the professor's head to a comfortable spot on the pillow or placing his glasses on the bridge of his nose. Kissing him good-bye earned you extra credit.

No books were required, yet many topics were covered, including love, work, community, family, aging, forgiveness, and finally, death. The last lecture was brief, only a few words."

Discussion Questions

• *What were some of your most memorable and favorite life lessons that Mitch learned from Morrie?*

• *Did Mitch change during his weekly visits with "coach"? If so, how?*

• *Morrie told his friends that if they really wanted to help him, they would treat him with visits, not sympathy. What did you learn from this statement, with respect to helping others who may be ill or otherwise suffering?*

• *What did you learn about the importance of parenthood, or what Morrie called "spiritual security", from Mitch and Morrie's fifth Tuesday talk? What did you learn from young Morrie's relationship with his father after his own mother's death and later, with his step mother, Eva?*

Interesting Facts

*Mitch David Albom was born on May 23, 1958, in Passaic, New Jersey to Ira and Rhoda Albom. His father worked as a corporate executive and his mother as an interior designer. He attended Brandeis University and graduated in 1979. He continued with his graduate work at Columbia University, and received his Masters Degree in 1982. He has worked as a news columnist/sports writer and talk show host for radio and television for over 20 years, including **The Mitch Albom Show**, a nationally syndicated sports talk show. While working as a staff writer for the Detroit Free Press, he introduced himself to his new readers saying they could expect, "some opinion, some heart, some frankness. Some laughs. Some out of the ordinary." He has also written several books on the subject, which include: **The Live Albom, Live Albom II, Live Albom III, Live Albom IV, and Gone to the Dogs**. He has received many award for his extensive work. He married Janine Sabino, a singer, in 1995. He gained huge success with his best-seller, **Tuesdays with Morrie: An Old Man, a Young Man, and Life's Greatest Lessons**, which has been described by Publisher's Weekly as "an emotionally rich book and a deeply affecting memorial to a wise mentor". It became the top-selling nonfiction book of 1998. It was also adapted to a television movie by Oprah Winfrey, which aired on ABC in 1999. Not only is Mitch incredibly talented in the sports and literary world, he is also an accomplished pianist, and composed a song for the television movie, **Christmas in Connecticut**, in 1992.*

"It was as if she had no preconditions...; the world simply unfolded before her, and she sustained the freedom always to be delighted."
John Forssen

Marshmallow Brownies

In a mixer, add:

1 CUP BUTTER (OR 1 CUBE BUTTER AND ½ CUP SHORTENING)
2 CUPS SUGAR
1/3 CUP COCOA

Beat well, then add:

4 EGGS (ADD 1 EGG AT A TIME AND BEAT WELL AFTER EACH EGG)
2 CUPS FLOUR (SIFTED)
2 TEASPOONS VANILLA

GREASE AND FLOUR A 9 X 13 PAN, POUR IN BATTER, AND BAKE AT 350 DEGREES FOR 30-35 MINUTES. INSERT A TOOTHPICK INTO THE CENTER OF THE PAN, IF IT COMES OUT CLEAN, THE BROWNIES ARE DONE. WHEN BROWNIES ARE DONE, TAKE PAN OUT OF OVEN AND POUR 6 CUPS OF MINI-MARSHMALLOWS ON TOP. TURN OVEN HEAT "OFF" AND RETURN PAN TO OVEN FOR 5 MINUTES, OR UNTIL THE MARSHMALLOWS START TO "PUFF" AND MELT TOGETHER. REMOVE FROM OVEN AND COOL COMPLETELY. WAIT UNTIL THE BROWNIES ARE COMPLETELY COOLED BEFORE FROSTING. IF YOU TRY TO FROST THE BROWNIES WHILE THEY ARE STILL EVEN A LITTLE WARM, YOU'LL GET SOMETHING THAT LOOKS LIKE A MISSISSIPPI MUD CAKE.

Frost with the following:

½ CUBE OF BUTTER
4 CUPS POWDERED SUGAR
1/3 CUP COCOA
1/3 CUP CANNED EVAPORATED MILK
2 TEASPOONS VANILLA

BROWNIES ARE BEST IF MADE THE DAY BEFORE THEY ARE SERVED. IF POSSIBLE WAIT UNTIL THE SECOND DAY TO FROST THEM, GIVING THE MARSHMALLOWS PLENTY OF TIME TO COOL. ALLOW SEVERAL HOURS FOR THE FROSTING TO SET UP BEFORE SERVING.

STANDING FOR SOMETHING
by
Gordon B. Hinckley

On marriage: *"There seems to be a superstition among many thousands of our young who hold and smooch in the drive-ins that marriage is a cottage surrounded by perpetual hollyhocks to which a perpetually young and handsome husband comes home to a perpetually young and ravishing wife. When the hollyhocks wither and boredom and bills appear, the divorce courts are jammed...Anyone who imagines that bliss is normal is going to waste a lot of time running around and shouting that he has been robbed...Life is like an old-time rail journey-delays, sidetracks, smoke, dust, cinders, and jolts, interspersed only occasionally by beautiful vistas and thrilling bursts of speed. The trick is to thank the Lord for letting you have the ride." Quoted from Jenkins Lloyd Jones*

On debt: *"Interest never sleeps nor sickens nor dies; it never goes to the hospital; it works on Sundays and holidays; it never takes a vacation; it never visit nor travels; it takes no pleasure; it is never laid off work nor discharged from employment; it never works on reduced hours;...it is as hard and soulless as a granite cliff. Once in debt, interest is your companion every minute of the day and night; you cannot shun it or slip away from it; you cannot dismiss it; it yields neither to entreaties, demands, or orders and whenever you get in its way or cross its course or fail to meet its demands, it crushes you."*
Quoted from J. Reuben Clark, Jr.

Discussion Questions

- *What was your favorite story told in the book? Why?*

- *Why do you think that the author claims that "love is the most enduring and most powerful virtue?"*

- *Of the ten virtues discussed in the book, which had the most powerful impact on you?*

- *On page 37, the author discusses a train that traveled 1,400 miles off course, due to a three inch mistake. Have you observed this principle at work in your own life, or in the lives of your friends and family? How?*

- *What is civility? Have you witnessed civility fading in our society?*

Interesting Facts

Gordon Bitner Hinckley was born June 23, 1910, in Salt Lake City, Utah, to Bryant S. and Ada Bitner Hinckley. He was a descendant of Stephen Hopkins who came to America on the Mayflower, and was the fourteenth signer of the Mayflower Compact. Another of his ancestors, Thomas Hinckley, was the governor of the Plymouth Colony. Unfortunately, Gordon was not a healthy child, and at the age of two was stricken with whooping cough. The illness left him weakened and susceptible to asthma and allergies during his childhood. Doctors told his worried parents, "The boy needs more fresh air and sunlight." They purchased a small farm outside of Salt Lake and spent weekends, holidays and summers enjoying the open air, and learning the value of hard work. As a young adult he served a mission for The Church of Jesus Christ of Latter Day Saints in England. Gordon found the work difficult with very little success, and wrote to his father, "I am wasting my time and your money, I don't see any point in my staying here." When his father's reply came, it simply read, "Dear Gordon, I have letter [of such and such date]. I have only one suggestion. Forget yourself and go to work. With Love, Your Father." He did, and his life's mission began. When Hinckley returned home from England, he was underweight, weary and had a desire "never to travel anywhere again." Now as the fifteenth president of The Church of Jesus Christ of Latter Day Saints, he has traveled more than 250,000 miles, circling the globe several times, teaching and inspiring the church's 12 million members.

He married Marjorie Pay (the cute girl who lived across the street) on April 29, 1937 in the Salt Lake Temple. Together the couple has five children,: Kathleen, Richard, Virginia, Clark and Jane. They also enjoy 25 grandchildren and many great-grandchildren. Marjorie states, "My husband taught by example. Throughout our married life I have never heard him lecture the children. They just knew what he expected of them because they watched him."

*Hinckley's book, **Standing for Something**, was published in 2000. It was listed on the Publisher's Weekly top 10 bestseller list, as well as the USA Today, Amazon.com and New York Times best sellers lists. Mike Wallace, of 60 Minutes, says of Hinckley, "He is a genuinely remarkable man. . . A warm and thoughtful and decent and optimistic leader."*

"To be happy: Don't do whatever you like; like whatever you do."
Anonymous

Chocolate-Cherry Stack-Ups

1 box Nabisco Nilla chocolate wafer cookies
6 ounce container of whipped topping, or whip your own cream
maraschino cherries, cut in half

The Basic Stack-up:

Start with one wafer; place a small dollop of whipped cream on top of it. Place another wafer on that. Repeat with whipped cream, cookie, then whipped cream again. Top with a cherry cut in half.

Arrange stacked wafers on a tray and place in a freezer. Freezing them overnight is best, but try to freeze for at least six hours. If you place them in an airtight container, they can be made several days ahead of time.

There are many fun variations you can try with these, including the following:

Crush candy canes or peppermint candies, and fold them into the whipped cream.
Divide the whipped cream in half and use food coloring to make red and green layers for Christmas.
Use candy sprinkles or edible glitter to decorate the top of each stack.

Each box of wafers contains about 40 cookies. You can make 13 three-layered cookies, or approximately 20 two-layered cookies.

THE SCREWTAPE LETTERS

by

C. S. Lewis

"You will say that these are very small sins; and doubtless, like all young tempters, you are anxious to be able to report spectacular wickedness. But do remember, the only thing that matters is the extent to which you separate the man from the Enemy. It does not matter how small the sins are provided that their cumulative effect is to edge the man away from Light and out into the Nothing. Murder is no better than cards if cards can do the trick. Indeed the safest road to Hell is the gradual one-the gentle slope, soft underfoot, without sudden turnings, without milestones, without signposts.
Your affectionate uncle, Screwtape"

Discussion Questions

- *Could you relate to any of the "daily pinpricks" that Screwtape suggested to Wormwood?*

- *Screwtape claims that he and his evil spirits had rescued thousands of humans annually. In modern Christianity, you find very few of the old warnings about "Worldly Vanities, the Choice of Friends, and the Value of Time". Such values are now viewed as "Puritanism". Screwtape stated, "May I remark in passing that the value we have given to that word is one of the really solid triumphs of the last hundred years." Do you agree with Screwtape? Why?*

- *In letter 14, Screwtape suggests, "I see only one thing to do at the moment. Your patient has become humble; have you drawn his attention to the fact? All virtues are less formidable to us once the man is aware that he has them, but this is specially true of humility. Catch him at the moment when he is really poor in spirit and smuggle into his mind the gratifying reflection, "By jove! I'm being humble," and almost immediately pride – pride at his own humility - will appear." Do you agree with this statement? If so, what evidences of this "tactic" have you witnessed?*

- *What do you think of the names that C.S. Lewis gave to the evil Spirits? Did they remind you of anything?*

- *Screwtape has another great idea for Wormwood's patient in letter 27: "Don't forget the 'heads I win, tails you lose' argument. If the thing he prays for doesn't happen, then that is one more proof that petitionary prayers don't work; if it does happen, he will, of course, be able to see some of the physical causes which led up to it, and 'therefore it would have happened anyway', and thus a granted prayer becomes just as good a proof as a denied one that prayers are ineffective." Does this argument sound familiar?*

Interesting Facts

Clive Staples Lewis was born on November 29, 1898 in Belfast, Northern Ireland. He was known to family and friends as "Jack" or "Jacks." He gave himself the nickname "Jacksie" when he was four years old and the name stuck.

Lewis attended University College, Oxford, where he started a writers club called, **The Inklings.** *The club would meet to share stories. J.R.R. Tolkien, who later wrote* **The Hobbit** *and* **The Lord of the Rings**, *was also a member. Tolkien was a very religious man and got Lewis thinking about Christianity. In 1929, he became a Christian. Lewis wrote his first religious book within four years of his conversion. This book was titled* **The Pilgrim's Regress**. *During World War II, he wrote several more books focusing on Christianity including* **The Screwtape Letters**, *which were dedicated to J.R.R. Tolkien.*

Lewis appeared on the cover of **Time** *magazine in 1947. The title of his autobiography,* **Surprised by Joy,** *took on new meaning in 1952 after he met and married American writer Joy Davidman. Lewis was broken hearted when Joy died from cancer in 1960. The movie* **Shadowlands** *is based on his life.*

More interesting facts on C. S. Lewis can be found on page 84.

"Great thoughts always come from the heart."
Marquis De Vauvenargues

Lemon Squares

Crust

½ CUP BUTTER, SOFTENED
1 CUP FLOUR
¼ CUP POWDERED SUGAR
¼ TEASPOON LEMON EXTRACT
A PINCH OF SALT

PREHEAT OVEN TO 350 DEGREES. BUTTER AN 8-INCH SQUARE PAN. CREAM ALL INGREDIENTS TOGETHER UNTIL SOFT AND SMOOTH. PRESS DOUGH INTO THE PAN. BAKE FOR 20 MINUTES. MAKE THE TOPPING WHILE THE CRUST IS BAKING.

Topping:

2 EGGS
1 CUP SUGAR
¼ TEASPOON LEMON EXTRACT
JUICE AND ZEST (GRATED OUTER PEEL) OF 1 LEMON
¼ CUP UNBLEACHED FLOUR
½ TEASPOON BAKING POWDER
POWDERED SUGAR FOR TOP

BEAT EGGS WELL, ADD SUGAR SPARINGLY UNTIL MIXTURE IS THICK. GRADUALLY ADD THE OTHER INGREDIENTS EXCEPT THE POWDERED SUGAR. CONTINUE BEATING UNTIL THE CRUST IS FINISHED COOKING. POUR MIXTURE OVER THE CRUST, AND RETURN TO THE OVEN. REDUCE HEAT TO 325 DEGREES. BAKE FOR 30-35 MINUTES, UNTIL GOLDEN. COOL FOR 20 MINUTES, CUT INTO SQUARES, AND THEN REMOVE FROM THE PAN. SIFT POWDERED SUGAR OVER THE SQUARES AND ENJOY!

THE COLOR OF WATER

by
James McBride

"I'm crying 'cause I'm happy. Anything wrong with that?" "No," I said, but there was, because happy people did not seem to cry like she did. Mommy's tears seemed to come from somewhere else, a place far away, a place inside her that she never let any of us children visit, and even as a boy I felt there was pain behind them. I thought it was because she wanted to be black like everyone else in church, because maybe God liked black people better, and one afternoon on the way home from church I asked her whether God was black or white.

A deep sigh. "Oh boy ... God's not black. He's not white. He's a spirit." "Does he like black or white people better?" "He loves all people. He's a spirit." "What's a spirit?" "A spirit's a spirit." "What color is God's spirit?" "It doesn't have a color," she said. "God is the color of water. Water doesn't have a color."

Discussion Questions

• *How did James McBride's childhood experiences compare to your own?*
• *What influence has your mother and family had in your life?*
• *Has reading this book changed or reaffirmed your opinions of the influence that parents have on their children?*
• *What is your opinion of Ruth's marriage? How are mixed race marriages viewed today? In your opinion, has society become more or less racially tolerant? What can you do to improve racial harmony?*

Interesting Facts

*James McBride was born in the 1950's and raised in the Red Hook housing projects in Brooklyn. He was the eighth of twelve children born to a black minister father and a white Jewish mother. James McBride has worked for The Boston Globe, People Magazine, Rolling Stone and The Washington Post. James' true passion, however, is music. He is an accomplished Jazz musician and composer. He has written songs for many talented performers including Anita Baker, Grover Washington Jr. and Gary Burton. He has even written children's songs for the PBS television show, **Barney and Friends**. He has toured with many artists including Michael Jackson and Little Jimmy Scott. James has also written award winning musicals for adults and children. **The Color of Water** took James McBride fourteen years to complete. The majority of that time was spent on research.*

*James has received criticism from both blacks and Jews for writing **The Color of Water**. To them he responds, "This book doesn't attack anyone, it just tells a story . . . I wrote it from a pure place . . . I hoped someone would get something out of it. I'm proud of my background . . . when you talk about race and religion in America you're always going to offend someone . . . What I've tried to do . . . is present my story in a pure way that would affect someone else in a pure way."*

*James' second book, a novel entitled **Miracle at St. Anna,** was recently released. He has also been selected to write the autobiography of Quincy Jones.*

"Treat your friends as you do your pictures, and place them in their best light."

Jennie Jerome Churchill

Seven Layer Bars

¼ CUP BUTTER
1 CUP GRAHAM CRACKER CRUMBS
1 ¼ CUP FLAKED COCONUT, DIVIDED
1 CUP CHOPPED WALNUTS
1 CUP SEMISWEET OR MILK CHOCOLATE CHIPS
1 CUP BUTTERSCOTCH CHIPS
1 CAN (14 OUNCES) SWEETENED CONDENSED MILK

PREHEAT OVEN TO 350 DEGREES. MELT BUTTER INTO A 9 X 9 INCH BAKING PAN IN THE OVEN. TILT PAN TO SPREAD THE BUTTER EVENLY. PRESS CRUMBS EVENLY INTO THE PAN. ADD LAYERS OF 1 CUP COCONUT, WALNUTS, CHOCOLATE CHIPS, BUTTERSCOTCH CHIPS, AND REMAINING COCONUT. DRIZZLE THE CONDENSED MILK OVER THE LAYERS. SHAKE THE PAN GENTLY TO EVEN THE LAYERS. BAKE FOR 30 MINUTES. LET COOL. USING A SHARP KNIFE, LOOSEN AROUND THE EDGES OF THE PAN. PLACE PAN IN THE REFRIGERATOR TO CHILL BEFORE CUTTING INTO SQUARES. TO SERVE A LARGER GROUP, YOU CAN DOUBLE THE RECIPE AND BAKE IT IN A 9 X 13 PAN. M&M MINIS ARE A FUN AND COLORFUL ALTERNATIVE TO THE CHOCOLATE CHIPS.

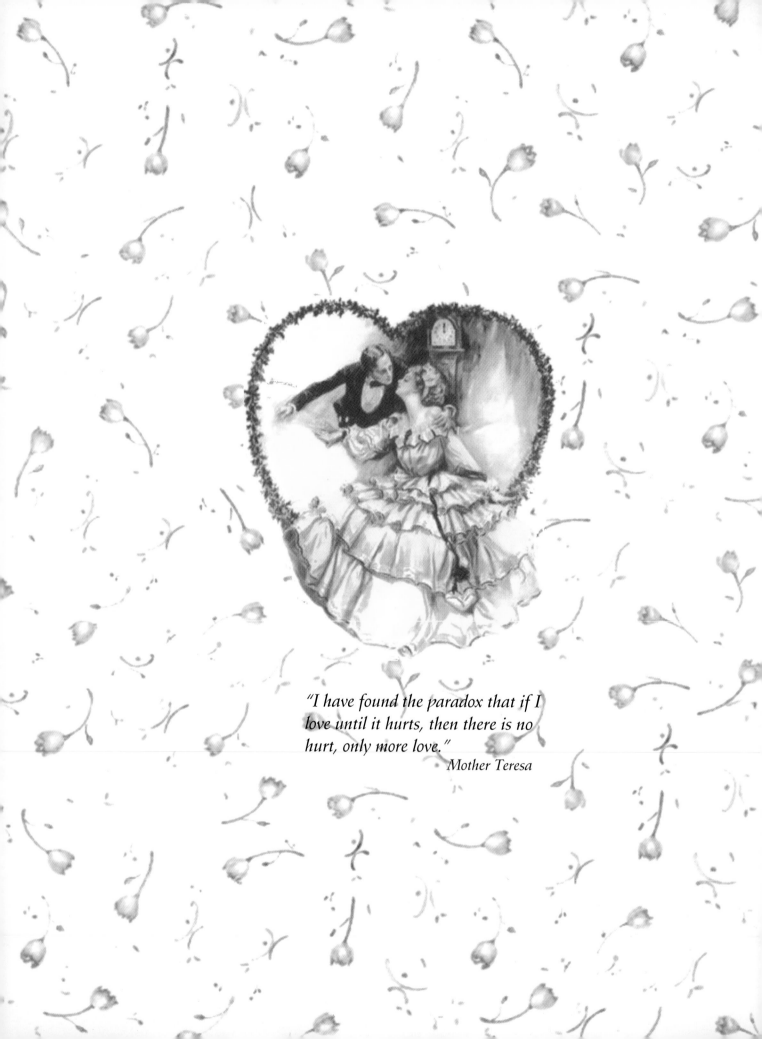

"I have found the paradox that if I love until it hurts, then there is no hurt, only more love."
Mother Teresa

February
LOVE STORIES

To all those hopeless romantics out there, this month is for you! The books in this month's section are full of intrigue, misconception, dashing damsels, brave men in disguise, daring rescues, family secrets and love conquering all. And if that is not enough to get you in the mood, the desserts we have chosen certainly will. Any one of these February books could make a very romantic Valentine's Day gift.

PRIDE AND PREJUDICE
by
Jane Austen

"You are mistaken, Mr. Darcy, if you suppose that the mode of your declaration affected me in any other way, than as it spared me the concern which I might have felt in refusing you, had you behaved in a more gentleman-like manner.' She saw him start at this, but he said nothing, and she continued, 'You could not have made me the offer of your hand in any possible way that would have tempted me to accept it.' Again his astonishment was obvious; and he looked at her with an expression of mingled incredulity and mortification. She went on. 'From the beginning, from the first moment I may almost say, of my acquaintance with you, your manners impressed me with the fullest belief of your arrogance, your conceit, and your selfish disdain of the feelings of others, were such as to form that groundwork of disapprobation, on which succeeding events have built so immovable a dislike; and I had not known you a month before I felt that you were the last man in the world whom I could ever be prevailed on to marry.'"

Discussion Questions

- *Discuss some of you favorite displays of pride and prejudice. Which characters exhibited the most?*

- *How did you feel about Mrs. Bennet and her tactics to see that her daughters married well?*

- *What characters did you despise the most? Who did you love the most?*

- *What changes came over Mr. Darcy as the story progressed? How about Elizabeth? How did their feelings for each other change?*

Interesting Facts

*Jane Austen was born on December 16, 1775 at Steventon, Hampshire, England. She was the seventh of eight children born to the Reverend George and Cassandra Austen. Her father was the local rector, and made a respectable income, which he helped to supplement by housing and tutoring pupils. He was by no means rich and like Mr. Bennet in her book, **Pride and Prejudice**, he could not have given his daughters "much to marry on."*

*The Austen children were taught mostly at home; the family had a vast library and they were all avid readers. Jane and her only sister, Cassandra, went briefly to a school in Southampton, but were sent home after an infectious disease broke out. They later attended the Abbey boarding school for one year. Over 100 letters between Jane and Cassandra have survived, giving an intimate look at their lives. **Pride and Prejudice** was sold in November of 1812, Jane calling it in a letter, "her own darling child". It was later published the following January. She sold the copyright for 110 pounds, and received nothing more for it. After the book was published, word of her great talent started to spread outside of her family circle. She wrote many highly prized novels, but received very little nominal gain from them. In 1817, Jane started on her final novel but had to give it up by March, being very ill. In April of that year, she made her will, leaving almost everything to her sister, Cassandra. Jane Austen died July 18, 1817, at the age of 41. The cause of her death is unknown, but is thought to have resulted from Addison's disease.*

More interesting facts on Jane Austen can be found on page 46.

"We can only learn to love by loving."

Iris Murdock

Pecan Cups with Raspberry Cheesecake Filling

Pecan Cups:

1 CUP CHOPPED PECANS
2/3 CUP TIGHTLY PACKED BROWN SUGAR
1 CUBE BUTTER
½ CUP LIGHT CORN SYRUP
2/3 CUP FLOUR

HEAT THE BROWN SUGAR, BUTTER AND CORN SYRUP OVER MEDIUM HEAT. BRING TO A BOIL AND THEN REMOVE FROM HEAT. ADD THE PECANS AND FLOUR. STIR THOROUGHLY WITH A WOODEN SPOON. SPRAY A COOKIE SHEET WITH NON-STICK SPRAY AND PLACE ONE HEAPING TABLESPOON OF BATTER AT EACH END OF COOKIE SHEET. THE BATTER WILL SPREAD OUT AND MAKE LARGE THIN ROUNDS, SO BE SURE TO ALLOW ENOUGH ROOM FOR THAT ON THE PAN. BAKE AT 325 DEGREES FOR 15 MINUTES. TAKE THE PAN OUT OF THE OVEN AND LET IT COOL FOR APPROXIMATELY TWO MINUTES. AS SOON AS THE ROUNDS ARE COOL ENOUGH TO PICK UP, AND FIRM ENOUGH TO WORK WITH, PICK UP WITH A SPATULA AND PLACE EACH ONE OVER A TEA CUP. PINCH DOWN THE SIDES OF THE ROUND TO FORM A CUP SHAPE. YOU HAVE TO WORK VERY QUICKLY, BECAUSE THE ROUNDS COOL. ONCE COOL, THE FORM WILL BE SET. THIS PROCESS TAKES SOME PRACTICE, SO DO NOT GIVE UP WITHOUT TRYING SEVERAL TIMES. THE "FLOPS" WILL STILL TASTE GREAT AND CAN BE BROKEN INTO PIECES AND SERVED OVER ICE CREAM. THESE ALSO WORK WELL AS ICE CREAM SUNDAE CUPS!

Cheesecake Filling:

8 OUNCE PACKAGE CREAM CHEESE
1 TEASPOON VANILLA
1 CUP POWDERED SUGAR
2 CUPS WHIPPED TOPPING (THAWED)

BEAT INGREDIENTS WELL WITH A HAND MIXER. USING A SPATULA, FOLD IN THE WHIPPED TOPPING. SPOON THE MIXTURE INTO COOLED PECAN CUPS.

Raspberry Sauce:

1 PACKAGE DANISH DESSERT
1 CUP FRESH OR FROZEN RASPBERRIES
OR
1 CAN RASPBERRY PIE FILLING TO SUBSTITUTE FOR BOTH OF THE ABOVE

PREPARE THE DANISH DESSERT AS DIRECTED ON THE PACKAGE FOR THE "FRUIT SAUCE." ALLOW IT TO COOL. THEN FOLD IN THE RASPBERRIES, AND SPOON THE MIXTURE OVER CHEESECAKE FILLING. YOU CAN ALSO ADD A DOLLOP OF WHIPPED TOPPING TO THE TOP.

THE SCARLET PIMPERNEL

by

Baroness Emmuska Orczy

"How strange it all was! She loved him still. And now that she looked back upon the last few months of misunderstandings and loneliness, she realized that she had never ceased to love him; that deep down in her heart she had always vaguely felt that his foolish inanities, his empty laugh, his lazy nonchalance were nothing but a mask; that the real man, strong, passionate, willful, was there; still-the man she had loved, whose intensity had fascinated her, whose personality attracted her, since she always felt that behind his apparently slow wits there was a certain something, which he kept hidden from all the world, and most especially from her."

Discussion Questions

- At what point did you realize the true identity of the Scarlet Pimpernel?
- Discuss the relationship between Sir Percy and Lady Blakeney? How does it evolve through the course of the book?
- Who would you name as the hero of the story? Why?
- Discuss the symbolism used by Baroness Orczy? (i.e., the "Chat Gris" and "The Fisherman's Rest")
- What political statements do you believe Baroness Orczy was making? Why?

Interesting Facts

Baroness Emmuska Orczy was born in Tarna-Ors, Hungary, in 1865 to Baron Felix and Emma Orczy. The Baron was a noted composer and conductor, who learned much from his father and his father's associates, Wagner, Liszt and Gounod. The Orczy family lived in Budapest, Brussels and Paris where the Baroness was educated in convent schools. They eventually moved to London and at the age of fifteen, she learned to speak English. Baroness Orczy studied at the West London School of Arts and the Heatherby School of Arts. It was at the latter that she met and married Montague Barstow. The Baroness was best known for her novel, **The Scarlet Pimpernel**, which was originally rejected by over a dozen publishers. She and her husband co-wrote a stage version of the book in 1903, which was very successful. They co-wrote two other plays, **The Sin of William Jackson** and **Beau Brocade**. Orczy was also a noted artist. Her works were exhibited at the Royal Academy in London. She and her husband also produced book and magazine illustrations, as well as a book of Hungarian folk tales entitled, **Old Hungarian Fairy Tales**.

Baroness Orczy and Montague moved to Monte Carlo during Hitler's regime. Montague died there in 1942. When World War II was over, the Baroness moved back to London where she worked actively into her 80's. She died in London on November 12, 1947

"My bounty is as boundless as the sea,
My love as deep; the more I give to thee
The more I have, for both are infinite."

Shakespeare

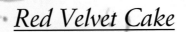 *Red Velvet Cake*

Two 1-ounce bottles of red food coloring
½ cup shortening
1 ½ cups sugar
2 eggs
2 heaping tablespoons cocoa
1 tablespoon vinegar
1 teaspoon salt
1 teaspoon vanilla
1 cup buttermilk
2 ¼ cups flour

Cake:

In a bowl, mix the shortening and sugar together until creamy. Add eggs and beat until smooth. Make a paste of the food coloring and cocoa in a small bowl and add to the creamed mixture. Mix the buttermilk, salt and vanilla together. Alternate adding a small portion of the buttermilk mixture and a portion of the flour to the creamy mixture. Repeat as necessary until it is all mixed together.

Mix the baking soda and the vinegar together in a separate bowl, and then fold into the cake batter. Grease and flour either two round pans or two heart-shaped pans. Add batter to the pans and bake at 350 degrees for 25-30 minutes.

Frosting:

3 heaping tablespoons flour
3/4 cup milk
1 cup sugar
1 teaspoon vanilla
½ cup butter

Cook the flour and milk until it is very thick, stirring constantly. Cool completely. With a mixer, cream the sugar, butter and vanilla together. Spoon in the cooled flour mixture, and continue to mix until creamy. Keep mixing until the ingredients have the consistency of whipped cream. If you find that it does not make enough frosting, you may want to either double the recipe or fold in one cup of whipped topping.

JANE EYRE
by
Charlotte Bronte

"Your name, little girl?" "Jane Eyre, sir." In uttering these words, I looked up: he seemed to me a tall gentleman; but then I was very little: his features were large, and they and all the lines of his frame were equally harsh and prim. "Well Jane Eyre, and are you a good child?" Impossible to reply to this in the affirmative; my little world held a contrary opinion: I was silent..." Come here," he said. I stepped across the rug, he placed me square and straight before him. What a face he had, now that it was almost on a level with mine! what a great nose! and what a mouth! and what prominent teeth! "No sight so sad as that of a naughty child," he began, "especially a naughty little girl." "Do you know where the wicked go after death?" "They go to hell," was my ready and orthodox answer. "And what is hell? Can you tell me that?" "A pit full of fire." "And should you like to fall into that pit, and to be burned there forever?" "No, sir." "What must you do to avoid it?" I deliberated a moment; my answer, when it did come, was objectionable: "I must keep in good health, and not die."

Discussion Questions

- *Discuss some of the hardships that Jane experienced during her childhood. Which ones broke your heart the most?*

- *What did you learn from the life of Jane Eyre?*

- *When did you first realize the identity of the horseman that Jane met in Hay Lane? What was your first impression of him? How did your impression change as the story progressed?*

- *What feelings did you have regarding the relationship between Rochester and Adele? Rochester and Bertha? Rochester and Jane?*

Interesting Facts

Charlotte Bronte was born in 1816 to the Rev. Patrick and Maria Bronte. She was the third daughter born, with a son and two more daughters to follow. Charlotte was born at Thornton in Yorkshire, but when she was four years old her father was appointed curate of Haworth, and it was there that the family spent the remainder of their lives. One year later, at the age of five, Charlotte's mother died. Charlotte and her sisters Maria, Elizabeth and Emily became students at the Clergy Daughter's School at Cowan Bridge at Lancashire. The same school that Charlotte would later describe in **Jane Eyre**. *One year later, unfortunately both Maria and Elizabeth died of consumption. Charlotte and Emily returned home. She later finished her schooling at Roe Head. She then returned home to tutor her sisters. In 1835, she was offered a teaching/governess position at Roe Head, but that only lasted one year. Charlotte also tried being a governess for two families, but again, after only a few months, she would return home. Charlotte, with the help of her two remaining sisters tried to start their own school in Haworth, but were unable to solicit any students. The sisters all loved to write, and in 1846, they published a book of poems under the pseudonyms of Currier, Ellis and Acton Bell. The following year, Charlotte's* **Jane Eyre** *was published (as well as Emily's* **Wuthering Heights** *and Anne's* **Agnes Grey**). *In 1848, their brother, by then an alcoholic and drug addict, died. Emily died that same year of consumption, and Anne, while nursing her sister, caught the disease, and died one year later. At the age of 33, Charlotte was left as the only living child. In 1849, Charlotte visited London and started moving in literary circles, and made the acquaintance of Thackeray. She attended many of his lectures and later dedicated* **Jane Eyre** *to him. After an on again/off again relationship with A.B. Nicholls, they married in 1854. Charlotte admired Nicholls, but never loved him. She became pregnant right away, but never delivered her child. During her pregnancy, she caught pneumonia and died only nine months after her marriage, at the age of 38. Her life was one of great sorrow and unbelievable tragedy.*

"There is no more lovely, friendly, and charming relationship, communion, or company than a good marriage."

Anonymous

Heavenly Cheesecake

2 CUPS GRAHAM CRACKER CRUMBS
1/3 CUP BUTTER, MELTED
1 ½ CUPS SUGAR PLUS 2 TABLESPOONS, DIVIDED
3 PACKAGES (8 OUNCES EACH) CREAM CHEESE, SOFTENED
4 EGGS
1 TEASPOON VANILLA EXTRACT
1 2/3 CUPS (OR A 10 OUNCE PACKAGE) OF VANILLA MILK CHIPS OR WHITE CHOCOLATE CHIPS

Cheesecake:

HEAT THE OVEN TO 350 DEGREES. IN A SMALL BOWL STIR TOGETHER THE GRAHAM CRACKER CRUMBS, BUTTER AND TWO TABLESPOONS OF SUGAR. PRESS THE MIXTURE INTO BOTTOM OF A 9-INCH SPRINGFORM PAN. BAKE FOR FIVE MINUTES OR UNTIL GOLDEN BROWN. REMOVE FROM OVEN. IN A LARGE BOWL, BEAT CREAM CHEESE AND THE 1 ½ CUPS SUGAR UNTIL SMOOTH. ADD EGGS AND VANILLA; BEAT WELL.

PLACE CHIPS IN A SMALL BOWL. MICROWAVE FOR 60 TO 90 SECONDS ON A HIGH SETTING, OR UNTIL CHIPS ARE MELTED AND SMOOTH WHEN STIRRED. BLEND MELTED CHIPS INTO THE CREAM CHEESE MIXTURE. POUR OVER THE CRUST. BAKE 35-40 MINUTES OR UNTIL ALMOST SET. REMOVE FROM OVEN AND PLACE ON A WIRE COOLING RACK. WITH A KNIFE, CAREFULLY LOOSEN THE CAKE FROM SIDES OF THE PAN. LET IT COOL COMPLETELY, THEN REMOVE THE SIDES OF THE SPRINGFORM PAN. REFRIGERATE UNTIL FIRM.

Chocolate Drizzle:

½ CUP SEMISWEET OR MILK CHOCOLATE CHIPS
1 TABLESPOON SHORTENING (NO BUTTER OR OIL)

MICROWAVE FOR 30 TO 45 SECONDS. STIR UNTIL SMOOTH. USING THE TIP OF A SPOON OR A PASTRY BAG, DRIZZLE THE MIXTURE ACROSS TOP OF CHEESECAKE. SERVE AND ENJOY.

"It began in mystery, and it will end in mystery,
but what a savage and beautiful country lies in between."

Diane Ackerman

March

MYSTERY MONTH

*M*ystery
*A*ccusation
*R*easoning
*C*onclusion
*H*air Raising

Sherlock Holmes

by

Sir Arthur Conan Doyle

What a lovely thing a rose is!" He walked past the couch to the open window and held up the drooping stalk of a moss-rose, looking down at the dainty blend of crimson and green. It was a new phase of his character to me, for I had never before seen him show any keen interest in natural objects. "There is nothing in which deduction is so necessary as in religion," said he, leaning with his back against the shutters. "It can be built up as an exact science by the reasoner. Our highest assurance of the goodness of Providence seems to me to rest in the flowers. All other things, our powers, our desires, our food, are all really necessary for our existence in the first instance. But this rose is an extra. Its smell and its colour are an embellishment of life, not a condition of it. It is only goodness which gives extras, and so I say again that we have much to hope from the flowers." *(From The Naval Treaty)*

Discussion Questions

• What quality did you most admire in Sherlock Holmes? What quality did you least admire?

• What are your feelings on the relationship between Watson and Holmes? Do you think of Watson as Holmes' student, friend, or partner in the detective work? Do you believe Watson is included in the story only as a narrator?

• What is your favorite Sherlock Holmes story? Why?

• What are your feelings about the author's decision to kill Sherlock Holmes? What are your feelings on Holmes' character being brought back to life?

Interesting Facts

Arthur Ignatius Conan Doyle was born in 1859 in Edinburgh, Scotland. He was the second of ten children born to Charles Altamont Doyle and Mary Foley Conan. Charles Doyle was a depressed artist working in civil service. In 1876, he was sent away to be treated for alcoholism and was later confined for life after developing epilepsy. Young Conan Doyle was still proud of his father and used some of his illustrations in his book, **A Study in Scarlet**. He displayed his father's work in his office and later in an exhibit in 1924. Mary Foley Conan loved to tell her children stories of brave and chivalrous knights. She believed it would give the family courage during their hard times. Arthur was her oldest son and was greatly inspired by her storytelling. The family took in a boarder, Dr. Bryan Waller, after their father was sent away. The rent from Dr. Waller helped to bring the family financial stability. Dr. Waller was only six years older than Arthur and helped to lead him into his own career in medicine. Conan Doyle struggled in his medical practice, which led him to writing in his spare time. The stories of **Sherlock Holmes** were the result. **A Study in Scarlet**, his first novel, was published in 1887. The character, Sherlock Holmes, became very popular, but Sir Arthur Conan Doyle disliked him and eventually killed him off in **His Last Bow**, which was published in 1893. The public was so outraged that it demanded that Conan Doyle bring him back. Sir Arthur strongly supported the building of the Channel Tunnel between England and France. He anticipated a war between England and Germany, and knew that the channel would make it impossible for Germany to block food shipments to Britain. He wrote his warnings in a story called **"Danger!"** which was published in July of 1914. It was largely ignored by the British, but unfortunately the Germans were thought to have taken ideas from the book when World War I broke out later that year. Conan Doyle was 55 years old at the time and was told that he was too old to enlist. Some thought that his war efforts were ridiculous, while others, including Winston Churchill, supported him. He claimed to be agnostic, despite his strong Catholic upbringing. He later became involved in spiritualism, where he participated in séances, hypnotism and investigations of hauntings. He feared that it would not be good for his reputation, but refused to give it up. He even made a believer out of Harry Houdini for a short while in the 1920's. Doyle clung to those beliefs until his death in 1930.

"Life's too mysterious....
Don't take it serious!

*Sting of the Bee Cake**

1 CUP BUTTER (NO SUBSTITUTES)

2/3 CUP SUGAR

2 EGGS

3 CUPS SIFTED FLOUR

3 TEASPOONS BAKING POWDER

1 TEASPOON SALT

½ CUP MILK

CAREFULLY CREAM THE BUTTER. GRADUALLY ADD THE SUGAR, WHILE CREAMING IT TOGETHER WITH THE BUTTER. BEAT ONE EGG AT A TIME INTO THE MIXTURES, AND CONTINUE BEATING UNTIL LIGHT AND FLUFFY. ADD SIFTED DRY INGREDIENTS ALTERNATELY WITH MILK. REPEAT UNTIL ALL OF THE INGREDIENTS ARE INCLUDED. SPOON THE BATTER INTO A WELL-GREASED, 9-INCH SPRINGFORM PAN.

Topping:

½ CUP BUTTER

½ CUP SUGAR

1 CUP FINELY CHOPPED ALMONDS

2 TABLESPOONS MILK

2 TEASPOONS VANILLA

MELT THE BUTTER IN A PAN ON THE STOVE. BLEND IN THE CHOPPED ALMONDS, SUGAR, MILK, AND VANILLA. BRING MIXTURE TO A BOIL. REMOVE FROM HEAT AND COOL SLIGHTLY. SPREAD CAREFULLY OVER BATTER. BAKE AT 375 DEGREES FOR 50 MINUTES. REMOVE FROM OVEN AND COOL. REMOVE FROM THE SPRINGFORM PAN.

Butter Cream Filling:

1 CUP BUTTER

2 EGG YOLKS

2 CUPS POWDERED SUGAR

2 TEASPOONS VANILLA

½ CUP RASPBERRY JAM

SOFTEN BUTTER. BEAT IN EGG YOLKS, POWDERED SUGAR, AND VANILLA. SPLIT CAKE INTO TWO LAYERS, HORIZONTALLY. SPREAD THE BUTTER CREAM FILLING OVER THE BOTTOM LAYER. COVER BUTTER CREAM WITH RASPBERRY JAM. VERY CAREFULLY REPLACE THE TOP LAYER OF THE CAKE. CUT INTO THIN SLICES AND SERVE. MAKES 16 TO 20 SERVINGS. (CAKE WILL CUT MORE EASILY IF PARTIALLY FROZEN.)

*FROM THE LION HOUSE COOKBOOK

REBECCA
by
Daphne de Maurier

"Rebecca, always Rebecca. Wherever I walked in Manderly, wherever I sat, even in my thoughts and in my dreams, I met Rebecca ... I should never be rid of Rebecca. Perhaps I haunted her as she haunted me ... I could fight the living but I could not fight the dead."

Discussion Questions

• Were you surprised by the outcome of the book? If so, what outcome had you expected? Were you pleased with the way the book ended?

• What were your first impressions of Maxim, Mrs. Danvers, and Rebecca? How did your first impressions change as the story unfolded?

• The name "Rebecca" was very prevalent in the story. What was the name of the second Mrs. de Winter, the narrator? Why the discrepancy?

• What are your predictions for the couple's future? What would you do?

Interesting Facts

Daphne du Maurier was born in Regent's Park in England in 1907. Her parents were both actors and her grandfather was a well known author. Despite the du Maurier's fame, Daphne lived a sheltered life as a child. Daphne began writing **Rebecca** while living abroad in Egypt. She struggled with the story and threw away her first 15,000 words before starting over with only the title remaining. She never thought the book would be successful stating, ". . . the ending is a bit brief and a bit grim." It became her most popular novel. **Rebecca** was published in 1938. Some 45,000 copies were printed in the first month of publication. Daphne's husband was a lieutenant colonel in the army and his small pay left Daphne feeling the burden of supporting the family financially. A successful novel and the later sale of the movie rights elated her. **Rebecca** was given mixed reviews by critics. The book was compared quite often to **Jane Eyre**, with some saying Daphne was merely a copycat writer, but the public still loved it. Daphne shunned the spotlight, preferring to live as a recluse. She had many internal struggles and finally died in 1989, having given up on life.

"The greatest pleasure in life is doing what people say you cannot do."
Walter Bagehot

Ice Cream Cake Roll

1 DARK CHOCOLATE CAKE MIX
5 EGGS
½ CUP WATER
1 BRICK OF VANILLA ICE CREAM
(OR OTHER FLAVOR OF YOUR CHOICE)

SPRAY THE BOTTOM OF A 11X17 JELLYROLL PAN WITH NON-STICK SPRAY. CUT A PIECE OF WAX PAPER TO FIT THE BOTTOM OF THE PAN. LAY THE WAX PAPER IN THE BOTTOM OF THE PAN AND THEN SPRAY THE TOP OF THE WAX PAPER. BEAT THE CAKE MIX, EGGS AND WATER UNTIL FLUFFY. POUR INTO A JELLYROLL PAN AND BAKE AT 350 DEGREES FOR 12 TO 15 MINUTES.

DAMPEN A CLEAN CLOTH AND LAY IT FLAT ON A COLD SURFACE. (YOU MAY ALSO USE A DRY CLOTH SPRINKLED WITH POWDERED SUGAR.) REMOVE THE PAN FROM THE OVEN. WHILE THE CAKE IS STILL WARM, CAREFULLY TURN THE PAN OVER AND ALLOW THE CAKE TO FALL ONTO THE DAMP CLOTH. REMOVE THE WAX PAPER. ROLL THE CAKE IN THE CLOTH, STARTING AT THE SHORT END.

ALLOW THE BRICK OF ICE CREAM TO SOFTEN AND THEN CUT THE ICE CREAM INTO 9 SLICES. AFTER THE CAKE HAS COOLED, UNROLL IT, LAY SLICED ICE CREAM ON TOP, AND SPREAD IT EVENLY TO COVER THE CAKE. GENTLY ROLL THE CAKE AGAIN. WRAP THE CAKE IN SARAN WRAP, AND THEN FOIL. PLACE IN THE FREEZER UNTIL THE ICE CREAM IS FROZEN AGAIN.

BEFORE SERVING, CUT THE CAKE INTO SLICES AND DRIZZLE WITH HOT FUDGE OR ANOTHER FAVORITE TOPPING.

GREAT EXPECTATIONS
by
Charles Dickens

"I am instructed to communicate to him," said Mr. Jaggers, throwing his finger at me sideways, "that he will come into a handsome property. Further, that it is the desire of the present possessor of that property, that he be immediately removed from his present sphere of life and from this place, and be brought up as a gentleman-in a word, as a young fellow of great expectations."...
"Now you are to understand, secondly, Mr. Pip, that the name of the person who is your liberal benefactor remains a profound secret."

Discussion Questions for Great Expectations

- What was one of your most memorable scenes with Pip and Miss Havisham?

- How did you feel about Estella and the way she treated Pip? How about the way that Miss Havisham was conditioning her in the manner she should treat the opposite sex?

- When did you start questioning the identity of Pip's real benefactor?

- What important lessons did Pip learn from Magwitch?

Interesting Facts

Charles John Huffman Dickens was born on the southern coast of England, on February 7, 1812. He was the second of eight children. Dickens loved to read as a child, and **Don Quixote** and **Robinson Crusoe** were among his favorite books. He married Catherine Hogarth in 1836. The couple had ten children in fifteen years. Dickens worked as a law clerk and in the newspaper business, but ultimately wanted to pursue acting. He was so successful as a reporter that he decided to keep writing, although he never lost his love for the theater. His "big break" came when asked by an up-and-coming publisher in 1836 to write the text for a series of comical drawings, portraying members of a cockney sporting club. **The Posthumous Papers of the Pickwick Club** were the result and they became, historically, one of the most successful publishing ventures in Britain. Despite earlier success, in periodicals, English and American book editions, and as a public lecturer, Dickens found it hard to pay for his vast living expenses. It was at this time, in 1860, that he wrote **Great Expectations**. The huge success of the novel proved to be just what Dickens needed. It is considered by many to be Dickens' best book.
More interesting facts on Charles Dickens can be found on pages 44, 108, and 112.

"Figuring out who you are is the whole point of the human experience."
Anna Quindlen

Death by Chocolate Cake

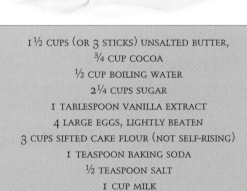

1 ½ CUPS (OR 3 STICKS) UNSALTED BUTTER,

¾ CUP COCOA

½ CUP BOILING WATER

2 ¼ CUPS SUGAR

1 TABLESPOON VANILLA EXTRACT

4 LARGE EGGS, LIGHTLY BEATEN

3 CUPS SIFTED CAKE FLOUR (NOT SELF-RISING)

1 TEASPOON BAKING SODA

½ TEASPOON SALT

1 CUP MILK

HEAT THE OVEN TO 350 DEGREES; ARRANGE TWO RACKS IN CENTER OF OVEN. SPRAY THREE 8-BY-2-INCH ROUND CAKE PANS WITH NON-STICK SPRAY; LINE THE BOTTOMS WITH WAX PAPER, SPRAY AGAIN. SIFT COCOA INTO A MEDIUM BOWL, AND WHISK IN A HALF CUP OF BOILING WATER. SET ASIDE TO COOL.

IN THE BOWL OF AN ELECTRIC MIXER FITTED WITH THE PADDLE ATTACHMENT, CREAM BUTTER ON LOW SPEED UNTIL IT IS LIGHT AND FLUFFY. GRADUALLY BEAT IN THE SUGAR UNTIL IT IS LIGHT AND FLUFFY, 3 TO 4 MINUTES, SCRAPING DOWN SIDES TWO TIMES. BEAT IN THE VANILLA. DRIZZLE IN EGGS, A LITTLE AT A TIME, BEATING BETWEEN EACH ADDITION UNTIL THE BATTER IS NO LONGER SLICK, SCRAPING DOWN THE SIDES TWO TIMES.

IN A LARGE BOWL, SIFT TOGETHER THE FLOUR, BAKING SODA, AND SALT. WHISK THE MILK INTO COOLED COCOA MIXTURE. WITH MIXER ON LOW SPEED, ALTERNATELY ADD THE FLOUR AND COCOA MIXTURE TO THE BATTER, A LITTLE OF EACH AT A TIME, STARTING AND ENDING WITH THE FLOUR MIXTURE.

DIVIDE THE BATTER EVENLY AMONG THE THREE PREPARED PANS. BAKE UNTIL A CAKE TESTER INSERTED INTO THE CENTER OF EACH LAYER COMES OUT CLEAN, USUALLY 35 TO 45 MINUTES. ROTATE THE PANS FOR EVEN BAKING. TRANSFER LAYERS TO WIRE RACKS FOR COOLING. WAIT 15 MINUTES. GENTLY REMOVE CAKES FROM PANS AND RETURN CAKES TO COOLING RACKS, TOP UP, AND ALLOW TO STAND UNTIL COMPLETELY COOLED. REMOVE PARCHMENT FROM BOTTOM OF EACH CAKE. SAVE THE SMOOTHEST LAYER FOR THE TOP.

Chocolate Ganache Icing:

24 OUNCES BITTERSWEET, SEMISWEET, OR MILK CHOCOLATE

3 CUPS HEAVY CREAM

CHOP THE CHOCOLATE INTO SMALL PIECES, AND PLACE INTO A MEDIUM BOWL. HEAT CREAM UNTIL BUBBLES BEGIN TO APPEAR AROUND THE EDGES (SCALDING); THEN POUR OVER THE CHOCOLATE. LET THE MIXTURE STAND FOR FIVE MINUTES, AND THEN STIR UNTIL SMOOTH. REFRIGERATE UNTIL COLD BUT NOT SOLID, STIRRING OCCASIONALLY. MAKES ABOUT 6 CUPS.

PLACE ONE CAKE LAYER ON A SERVING PLATTER AND SPREAD 1 ½ CUPS OF THE ICING OVER THE TOP. ADD THE SECOND CAKE LAYER, AND SPREAD WITH ANOTHER 1 ½ CUPS OF ICING. TOP WITH THIRD CAKE LAYER. COVER OUTSIDE OF CAKE WITH THE REMAINING 3 CUPS ICING. SERVE AND ENJOY.

DROWNING RUTH

by

Christina Schwarz

"Ruth remembered drowning. `That's impossible,' Aunt Amanda said. `It must have been a dream.' But Ruth maintained that she had drowned, insisted on it for years, even after she should have known better."

Discussion Questions

- *In your opinion, who is the heroine of the book? Why?*
- *Whose best interest was Amanda serving; Mathilda's, Ruth's, Imogene's or her own?*
- *If you could change one event in the story, what would it be and why? What effect would this change have had on the lives of the other characters?*
- *What were your feelings about the location where Ruth chose to stay? What would you have done if faced with the same situation?*

Interesting Facts

Christina Schwarz was born in Wisconsin. She spent her early life living with her family in a boathouse on Pewaukee Lake. The boathouse was originally the bathhouse of her great-great-grandfather's summer home. She received her undergraduate and Master's degrees from Yale University. In 1986, she married Benjamin Schwarz, a magazine editor. The couple moved many times, from England to Washington D.C., to Los Angeles and New York. Christina taught English at private schools in both Washington D.C. and Los Angeles. She quit teaching to begin writing a novel, and spent the next five years working on **Drowning Ruth**. **Drowning Ruth** is set on a Wisconsin lake similar to Pewaukee Lake. The story takes place in 1919, but the author drew upon several of her own childhood memories to set the stage and to develop the story. Christina had a mysterious neighbor while growing up whom she nicknamed, "the recluse." This women became the inspiration for **Drowning Ruth**, but was quickly overtaken by the characters of Amanda and Ruth. This book, the author's first novel, became a bestseller in 2000, and received many positive reviews, including a place on Oprah's Book Club list. Miramax Studios has announced its plans to bring the story to the big screen, in a movie that will be directed by Wes Craven. Schwarz was hoping to make enough money from her debut novel to justify writing another one. She was happily caught off guard by the success of **Drowning Ruth**.

"Neglect not the gift that is in thee."

Coconut Cream Cake

1 YELLOW CAKE MIX
1 LARGE VANILLA INSTANT PUDDING
1 1/3 CUPS WATER
4 EGGS
¼ CUP OIL
2 CUPS COCONUT (YOU WILL NEED A 14 OZ. BAG OF COCONUT FOR THIS RECIPE)
1 CUP CHOPPED WALNUTS

BLEND TOGETHER THE CAKE MIX, WATER, OIL, EGGS AND THE PUDDING. BEAT FOR 3 TO 4 MINUTES. THE PUDDING IN THE BATTER WILL MAKE THE BATTER VERY THICK AND CREAMY STIR IN COCONUT AND WALNUTS. GREASE AND FLOUR TWO ROUND CAKE PANS. ADD THE BATTER AND BAKE AT 350 DEGREES FOR 35 MINUTES.

Frosting:

4 TABLESPOONS BUTTER (AT ROOM TEMPERATURE)
1½ CUPS COCONUT
8 OUNCES CREAM CHEESE (AT ROOM TEMPERATURE)
2 TEASPOONS MILK
3 TO 3 1/2 CUPS POWDERED SUGAR
½ TEASPOON VANILLA

WITH A HAND MIXER, MIX TOGETHER ALL OF THE INGREDIENTS, EXCEPT FOR THE COCONUT. CONTINUE MIXING UNTIL SMOOTH. STIR IN COCONUT. FROST BETWEEN THE LAYERS AND AROUND THE OUTSIDE OF THE CAKE. AFTER FROSTING THE CAKE, PUT THE REMAINING COCONUT IN A SHALLOW PAN (A CAKE PAN OR PIE PLATE) AND TOAST IN THE OVEN UNTIL THE COCONUT IS LIGHTLY BROWN. WHEN THE COCONUT IS COOL, SPRINKLE IT ON TOP OF THE CAKE.

"One sure window into a person's soul is his reading list."

Mary B. W. Tabor

April
TEA PARTY MONTH

Lace table cloths, pretty dishes and dainty food may not be everyone's "cup of tea", but they should be, in concept at least. How much happier would we be if we each took a moment now and then to quietly enjoy the company of others and to relish in the presentation as well as the flavor of food? Reading a good book together is merely the "frosting on the cake"!

COLD SASSY TREE
by
Olive Ann Burns

"Now what I come to say," he blurted out, is that I'm aimin' to marry Miss Love Simpson." Mama's and Aunt Loma's mouths dropped open and their faces went white. They both cried out, "Pa, you cain't!" "I done ast her and she's done said yes. And Loma, there ain't a bloomin' thang you can do bout it." Aunt Loma's face got as red as if she'd been on the river all day, but it was Mama who finally spoke. In a timid voice she said, "Sir, Love Simpson's young enough to be your daughter! She's not more'n thirty-three or four years old!" "Thet ain't got a thang to do with it." Mama put both hands up to her mouth. With a sort of a whimper, she said, "Pa, don't you care what folks are go'n to say¿" "I care bout you carin' what they'll say, Mary Willis. But I care a heap more bout not bein' no burden on y'all. So hesh up." Aunt Loma was about to burst. "Think, Pa!" she ordered, tears streaming down her face, "Just think. Ma hasn't been d-dead but three w-w-weeks!" "Well good gosh a'mighty!" he thundered. "She's dead as she'll ever be, ain't she¿ Well, ain't she¿"

Discussion Questions

• *Would you want to live in Cold Sassy¿ Why¿*

• *How would you react if your own father made the same "announcement" as Mr. Blakeslee did at the beginning of the book¿*

• *What, if anything, did this book teach you about gossiping¿ Class distinction¿ Family relationships¿ Religious hypocrisy¿*

• *Discuss the advantages and disadvantages of the "mourning rituals" adhered to in Cold Sassy¿*

Interesting Facts

*Olive Ann Burns was born July 17, 1924 in Banks County, Georgia. Her father, William, was a farmer's cooperative executive, and her mother, Ruby, was a homemaker. She attended both Mercer University and University of North Carolina at Chapel Hill. In 1956, she married Andrew H. Sparks, an editor, and they had two children, Rebecca Marie and John Andrew. Olive spent eleven years working as a staff writer and free lance journalist for several Georgia companies and newspapers. From 1960-1967, she authored a local newspaper advice column "Ask Amy" under the pseudo name, Amy Larkin. Olive began writing **Cold Sassy Tree** in 1975. She had just been diagnosed with cancer and wanted to try her hand at writing a novel. It took her eight and a half years to complete the story, as she battled the terrible effects of chemotherapy. Much of her inspiration for the character, Grandpa Blakeslee, she gleaned from her Great Grandfather Power. He too, after being recently widowed, announced "he had to git him another wife or hire a housekeeper . . . and it would jest be cheaper to git married." He then married a much younger women. Olive began writing the sequel, **Leaving Cold Sassy**, but unfortunately it was left unfinished after her death from cancer on July 4, 1990. The fifteen chapters that she had finished were still published, even though the plot lines and character developments were incomplete. Although Burns was limited to two works, her colorful characters, detail-driven use of settings, and humor-laced plots endeared her to readers. She was inspired by what she knew best - the idiosyncrasies of her own family history.*

"The future belongs to those who believe in the beauty of their dreams."
Eleanor Roosevelt

Cherry Delights

2 EGGS

3/4 CUP SUGAR

1-2 TEASPOON FRESH LEMON JUICE

TWO 8 OUNCE PACKAGES CREAM CHEESE

1 TEASPOON VANILLA

1 TEASPOON LEMON ZEST

VANILLA WAFERS

CHERRY PIE FILLING (OR ANOTHER FLAVOR OF YOUR CHOICE)

LINE A CUP CAKE TIN WITH PAPER CUP CAKE LINERS. PLACE A VANILLA WAFER IN THE BOTTOM OF EACH CUP CAKE LINER. BEAT THE FIRST FIVE INGREDIENTS TOGETHER WELL AND POUR MIXTURE OVER EACH VANILLA WAFER. YOU CAN MAKE THEM AS THICK OR THIN AS YOU WISH. BAKE AT 350 DEGREES FOR 10-20 MINUTES. THE SIDES OF THE CHEESECAKE WILL LOOK SET. TURN THE OVEN OFF AND LEAVE CHEESECAKES IN FOR AN ADDITIONAL 30 MINUTES. REFRIGERATE UNTIL READY TO SERVE. YOU MAY SERVE THE CHEESECAKES IN OR OUT OF THE CUPCAKE LINERS. TOP WITH FRUIT BEFORE SERVING.

A Tale of Two Cities
by
Charles Dickens

"It was the best of times, it was the worst of times, it was the age of wisdom, it was the age of foolishness, it was the epic of belief, it was the epic of incredulity, it was the season of Light, it was the season of Darkness, it was the spring of hope, it was the winter of despair, we had everything before us, we had nothing before us, we were all going direct to heaven, we were all going direct the other way..."

Discussion Questions

• *A Tale of Two Cities has been described as a stark, moody and dark novel. What do you believe gives it that feel, and why do you think Dickens made it so dark and depressing?*

• *Compare the relationship between Lucie and Charles Darney, and the love he had for her, versus the love that Sydney Carton had for her? Did your feelings for Carton change as the story progressed? Why do you think Carton had Darney write the note to Lucie at the end of the story?*

• *After disliking Jerry Cruncher throughout the novel, how did you feel when Dickens redeemed him at the end of the story? Did you find it believable?*

• *Discuss some of the differences, and maybe a few similarities, between Miss Pross and Madame DeFarge. Do you think Madame DeFarge got what was coming to her, or do you think something else would have been more appropriate? If so, what?*

Interesting Facts

*Charles John Huffman Dickens was born in southern England, on February 7, 1812. His life was greatly changed by his experience of working in a blacking warehouse when he was twelve years old. Instead of letting it ruin his life and turn him into a vagabond, he turned to the reading of his favorite childhood books to keep his imagination alive and continue the vision of seeing himself moving beyond that horrible environment. He also kept alive the imaginations of the other boys working with him in the warehouse. Most of the other boys were uneducated and loved to hear Dickens retell the stories he had read. **A Dinner at Poplar Walk** was Dickens' first published story. It was printed in December of 1833. He had great success with his short stories but they were overshadowed by the even greater success of his novels. Dickens never thought of short stories as being a complete work of art anyway. The idea of **A Tale of Two Cities** came to him while he was performing in a play in Manchester in August of 1857. He was portraying a dying Richard Wardour and before the scene was over he was crying, together with two thousand audience members. He knew he needed to write a story about a great, honorable sacrifice, that would leave people in tears. By March 1858, **A Tale of Two Cities** was well under way. It was first published as a weekly serial and received the highest praise. Dickens said it was, "The best story I have written." It is believed the characters of Sydney Carton and Charles Darney are autobiographical. Dickens created the characters from internal conversations he was having with himself. The character of Lucie Manette is said to be based on Dickens' childhood friend, Lucy Stroughill, as well as on Ellen Ternan, the actress for whom he left his wife.*

More interesting facts on Charles Dickens can be found on pages 36, 108, and 112

"Most folks are about as happy as they make up their minds to be."

Abraham Lincoln

Sun Dried Tomato and Basil Butter

1/3 CUP MARINATED SUN DRIED TOMATOES
(DRAINED ON A PAPER TOWEL, THEN CUT INTO SMALL PIECES)
½ CUP BUTTER (AT ROOM TEMPERATURE)
1 OR 2 CLOVES GARLIC (MINCED)
2 TEASPOONS DRIED SWEET BASIL

BLEND ALL INGREDIENTS WELL, UNTIL THE BUTTER TURNS A SOFT RED COLOR, AND CHILL UNTIL READY TO SERVE. SERVE ON FRESH FRENCH BREAD OR SOUR DOUGH BREAD, TOPPED WITH YOUR FAVORITE CHEESE. THE SANDWICHES TASTE GREAT IF THEY ARE TOASTED UNDER THE BROILER TO SERVE WITH YOUR FAVORITE ENTREE.

MANSFIELD PARK
by
Jane Austen

"How could she have excited serious attachment in a man, who had seen so many, and been admired by so many, and flirted with so many, infinitely her superiors-who seemed so little open to serious impressions, even where pains had been taken to please him-who thought so slightly, so carelessly, so unfeelingly on all such points-who was every thing to every body, and seemed to find no one essential to him?... Every thing might be possible rather than serious attachment or serious approbation of it towards her. She had quite convinced herself of this before Sir Thomas and Mr. Crawford joined them. The difficulty was in maintaining the conviction quite so absolutely after Mr. Crawford was in the room; for once or twice a look seemed forced on her which she did not know how to class among the common meanings; in any other man at least, she would have said that it meant something very earnest, very pointed. But she still tried to believe it no more than what he might often have expressed towards her cousins and fifty other women."

Discussion Questions

• *How was Fanny's life different after going to live with her aunt, uncle and cousins?*
• *In your opinion, what situations caused Fanny's personality to be so different from her cousins, Julia and Maria? How did Edmunds' personality fit in with the mix?*
• *What were your feelings for the Crawford family? Do you think they would have made good marriage partners?*
• *The author's writing style has been described by critics saying that she "rewards the deserving and punishes the undeserving." Would you agree with this critique?*
• *Were you pleased with the ending? Why?*

Interesting Facts

Jane Austen was born December 16, 1775 at Steventon, Hampshire, England, to Reverend George and Cassandra Austen. Her father was the local rector for the Church of England. She was the seventh child of eight born to the couple, six sons and two daughters. Jane's older and only sister, Cassandra, was her best friend and confidant. Over 100 letters written between the two sisters were preserved, showing great details from their lives. In 1782, the Austen family started staging small plays at the Steventon rectory, and as the years pressed forward their productions became more elaborate. It is interesting to note that Jane displayed strong disapproval for amateur theatricals in **Mansfield Park**, which was written about 20 years later. It appeared on shelves in May 1814, was a huge success and sold out in six months. Mrs. Mitford, perhaps a jealous acquaintance, wrote that, "Jane was the prettiest, silliest, most affected, husband hunting butterfly I ever remember." Unfortunately, neither Jane nor Cassandra ever married, and there is little evidence of even a serious relationship for Jane. She did write at one time to Cassandra, "Friday - At length the day is come on which I am to flirt my last with Tom Lefroy, and when you receive this it will be over. My tears flow at the melancholy idea." Years later, Tom confessed to his nephew that he had had a "boyish love" for Jane. In December of 1801, Jane and Cassandra were staying with the Bigg Family at Manydown, which was near Steventon. One of their sons, Harris Bigg-Wither, who was six years younger than Jane, proposed to her, and she accepted. She recanted soon afterwards, having thought better and knowing that she did not love him. It was later revealed that Austen thought Harris to be, "big and awkward." Jane then escaped the situation with Cassandra, and they hurriedly left for Bath. Although socially embarrassing, the incident did not seem to affect Jane much. Jane Austen died on July 18, 1817, at the age of 41. She was buried at Winchester Cathedral, and since women at that time did not attend funerals, Cassandra was not present. A portion of the inscription on the memorial plaque on her grave reads, "She opened her mouth with wisdom and in her tongue is the law of kindness."

More interesting facts on Jane Austen can be found on page 22.

"If you can imagine it, you can achieve it, If you can dream it, you can become it."

Anonymous

Cucumber Sandwiches

½ English cucumber (if you substitute with a regular
cucumber, remove the seeds if they are large)
8 ounces cream cheese (at room temperature)
1 teaspoon lemon juice
2 teaspoons dill weed
salt and pepper to taste

✦

Grate one-half of the cucumber and drain the excess liquid. Mix all the ingredients together thoroughly. Top each piece of bread with a spoonful of mixture. Thinly slice the remaining half of the cucumber. Cut each cucumber slice in half, and lay it on top of the mixture.

Be creative with your bread selections. You can always use regular bread (with the crusts cut off), or try decorative bread tubes. (Pampered Chef has some fun ones.) You may also want to try individual size loaves, or even soup cans or larger size cans work as well; simply wash and dry the can, spray inside well with non-stick spray, add dough and bake, it will easily shake out after cooling for a couple of minutes. Use your favorite bread recipe, or pick up some frozen or refrigerated bread dough from the store.

A Tree Grows in Brooklyn

by

Betty Smith

"The one tree in Francie's yard was neither a pine nor a hemlock. It had pointed leaves which grew along green switches which radiated from the bough and made a tree which looked like a lot of opened green umbrellas. Some people called it the Tree of Heaven. No matter where its seed fell, it made a tree which struggled to reach the sky. It grew in boarded-up lots and out of neglected rubbish heaps and it was the only tree that grew out of cement. It grew lushly, but only in the tenement districts."

Discussion Questions

• *What were your feelings about Francie's mother, Katie, and her father Johnny? How were these feelings influenced by Johnny's drinking problem? How did Johnny's alcoholism affect each member of the Nolan family?*

• *After reading the story of Francie's grandmother, Mary Rommely, what were your feelings on education and literacy? How have education and literacy affected your life?*

• *Which characters did you admire the most and why? What do you feel was their greatest achievement?*

• *Upon it's release in 1943,* **A Tree Grows in Brooklyn** *faced criticism for being daring, pro-union, lascivious and too sympathetic to the poor. What are your feelings? How would these criticisms be regarded by today's standards?*

Interesting Facts

Elizabeth Wehner, the daughter of German immigrants, was born December 15, 1896, five years earlier than her beloved character Francie Nolan. "Betty" grew up poor in the Williamsburg section of Brooklyn, something she and Francie also shared. Betty married young and postponed her own formal education to raise her daughters. Once her children were in school, she began taking journalism, drama, writing and literature classes at a university despite having never finished high school. After working for a Detroit newspaper, reading plays, acting and writing her own plays, she published **A Tree Grows in Brooklyn** *in 1943, the same year that she married her second husband. The book sold over 300,000 copies in the first six weeks. The success of the book led her to write for the* **New York Times Magazine** *where she also addressed social issues. She received many awards as a dramatist and wrote three more novels, but never received the same attention or recognition as she did with* **A Tree Grows in Brooklyn. A Tree Grows in Brooklyn** *was chosen by the New York Public Library in 1995 as one of the "Books of the Century" and by Oprah Winfrey as one of the ten books that have greatly influence her life. The film rights were sold to Twentieth Century Fox for $55,000. James Dunn played the role of Johnny and won an Oscar for his performance. Betty died in 1972 claiming to have never had any intention of writing a book of "social significance."*

"I stir wild honey into my carefully prepared tea and wait for meaning to arise, to greet and comfort me."

Paula Gunn Allen

Miniature Tarts

You can do this either one of two ways (depending on the kind of day you're having!)

Crazy Day Method:

1 PKG. READY MADE PIE CRUST

20 OZ. CAN OF PIE FILLING (ANY FLAVOR YOU CHOOSE)

Cut the pastry into a circle, using a cookie cutter or the top of a glass, whichever will make the pastry fit into the miniature tart pan the best. Fill pastry lined cups with the pie filling; one 20 oz. can fills 24 miniature tarts. Bake at 350 degrees until pastry browns, which will take approximately 20 minutes.

Relaxed Day Method:

Pastry

4 CUPS FLOUR (SIFTED)

1 ¾ CUP SHORTENING

1 TABLESPOON SUGAR

2 TEASPOONS SALT

Combine the flour, sugar, and salt and then cut shortening into mixture until it resembles cornmeal texture.

In a small bowl, beat together:

1 EGG

1 TABLESPOON VINEGAR

½ CUP ICE COLD WATER

Combine the two mixtures together with a fork. Mix with your hands lightly, just until it forms a ball. Chill in the refrigerator for 15 minutes. Follow directions as above.

Peach Pie Filling

4 CUPS SLICED PEACHES

¼ CUP INSTANT TAPIOCA

¾ CUP SUGAR

1 TABLESPOON LEMON JUICE

Apple Pie Filling

6 CUPS PEELED, CORED AND SLICED APPLES

2 TABLESPOONS INSTANT TAPIOCA

¾ CUP SUGAR

½ TEASPOON CINNAMON

¼ TEASPOON NUTMEG

Mix all ingredients together and spoon into pie pastry

"You have to ask children
and birds how cherries and
strawberries taste."

Goethe

May

ADVENTURE MONTH

With the kids almost out of school and summer just around the corner, it is easy during the month of May for our minds to wander towards the vacations we are hoping to take and the adventures we are hoping to have. For some, traveling to exotic isles and distant lands will become a reality. For others, sandy beaches and daring exploits will have to be viewed, or read about, from the comfort of a living room sofa. Whatever your situation, we hope the books featured in this section will help quench your thirst for adventure, at least for the time being.

THE THREE MUSKETEERS

by

Alexandre Dumas

"And now, gentlemen," said D'Artagnan,... "All for one and one for all – that is our motto, is it not?"

"And yet..," said Porthos.

"Hold out your hand and swear!" cried Athos and Aramis at once. Overcome by example, grumbling to himself, nevertheless, Porthos stretched out his hand, and the four friends repeated with one voice the formula dictated by D'Artagnan:

"All for one, and one for all."

Discussion Questions

• Dumas has been called one of the best adventure story tellers of all time. Which "swashbuckling" adventure in **The Three Musketeers** was your favorite? Why?

• **The Three Musketeers** is known as a great novel of romance. How did you feel about the love and romance in this book? How did you feel about the relationship of Anne of Austria, Queen of France and the Duke of Buckingham? What did you think of the relationship between D'Artagnan and Constance?

• Athos, Porthos and Aramis, the three famous "King's Musketeers", are most often thought of collectively, yet they were all very different. Discuss each one's personality and vices.

• How did you feel about Milady? Were you surprised when you found out who she once had been?

Interesting Facts

Alexandre Dumas was born on July 24, 1802 to Thomas-Alexandre and Marie-Louise-Elisabeth Labouret Dumas. He was the youngest of three children. Alexandre's father died when he was only four years old. The family was left in financial straights. As a young boy, he did not receive much of a formal education because it was more important that he worked to help support his family. By the age of 22, he had produced several melodramas with the help of a friend, Adolphe de Leuven. He also had one of many affairs and on July 27, 1824, his son, Alexandre, was born. Another affair brought him a daughter, Marie-Alexandrine. To almost everyone's surprise, he was finally married to a women named Ida Ferrier. Ida loved Alexandre's daughter Marie, but hated young Alexandre, and young Alexandre felt the same about her. They were divorced after three years. In 1847, Dumas became the proprietor of a theater, which he dedicated to the performance of his own works. About this same time he had a great mansion built, the Chateau de Monte-Cristo. He invited 600 guests to his house warming party. The mansion was soon filled with scavenger friends, who were a tremendous drain on his finances, which also affected the upkeep of the theater. Soon the theater folded and he was forced into bankruptcy. Under pressure from creditors who were threatening to put him in jail, Dumas exiled to Brussels on December 10, 1851. He frequently socialized with Victor Hugo who had also exiled to Belgium because of his opposition to Napoleon III. Dumas finally reached an agreement with his creditors and returned to Paris in 1853. He had one more child, daughter Micaella-Josepha, as a result of an affair with a young aspiring actress. At the age of 68, tired and ill, he went to live with his son's family, and died at their home on December 5, 1870. He wrote 1,200 volumes in his life time and it is said that no one has read the complete works of Alexandre Dumas. He was best known for **The Three Musketeers** and **The Count of Monte Cristo.**

"No matter where I serve my guests, it seems they like my kitchen best."

Anonymous

Strawberry Spinach Salad with Poppy Seed Dressing

1 6 OUNCE BAG OF FRESH BABY SPINACH
1 POUND STRAWBERRIES (WASHED AND SLICED)
3-4 GREEN ONIONS (WASHED AND THINLY SLICED)
2 TABLESPOON SESAME SEEDS (TOASTED IN OVEN UNTIL LIGHTLY BROWN)
½ CUP SLIVERED ALMONDS

Dressing:

½ CUP OLIVE OIL
¼ CUP RED WINE VINEGAR
¼ CUP SUGAR
¼ TEASPOON PAPRIKA
1 TABLESPOON POPPY SEEDS

MIX ALL INGREDIENTS TOGETHER. REFRIGERATE UNTIL READY TO USE. YOU CAN SERVE THE DRESSING ON THE SIDE OR TOSS DRESSING AND SALAD TOGETHER IMMEDIATELY BEFORE SERVING.

ROBINSON CRUSOE

by

Daniel Defoe

"I frequently sat down to my meat with thankfulness, and admired the hand of God's providence which had thus spread my table in the wilderness, I learned to look more upon the bright side of my condition and less upon the dark side; and to consider what I enjoyed rather than what I wanted; and this gave me sometimes such secret comforts that I cannot express them; and which I take notice of here, to put those discontented people in mind of it who cannot enjoy comfortably what God has given them because they see and covet something that He has not given them. All our discontents about what we want appeared to me to spring from the want of thankfulness for what we have."

Discussion Questions

• *What would be the hardest thing to face if you were stranded on an island: loneliness, vulnerability, absence of luxury, physical strain, or monotony?*

• *Robinson Crusoe was very resourceful in using objects on the island. What was his most clever invention?*

• *How would Robinson Crusoe's experience have been different if one of his shipmates had survived the ship wreck?*

• *How did Robinson Crusoe's life change after his experience on the island? How did it stay the same? What was his greatest lesson learned?*

Interesting Facts

*Daniel Defoe was born in England in 1660 to James and Alice Foe. Defoe's father, a butcher, had always hoped his son would enter the ministry, but Defoe had dreams of other things. He had his first taste of writing while attending an academy, which was run by Charles Morton. The students were often asked to write letters to and from fictional characters. Defoe married Mary Tuffley on January 1, 1684, which proved to be the beginning of a tumultuous life together. They had eight children together. He left in June of 1685 to join a rebellion against King James II. Defoe was always at the forefront of politics and his political writing often put him in difficult situations. Daniel had more than eight lawsuits filed against him during his lifetime. He declared bankruptcy twice, and was twice imprisoned. He also spent approximately seven months in hiding. He dappled in everything from politics and investments, to making perfume from cat urine. **The Life and Strange Surprising Adventures of Robinson Crusoe, of York, Mariner** and it's sequel, **The Farther Adventures of Robinson Crusoe: Being the Second and Last Part of His Life** were published in 1719. They have been read all over the world, bringing Defoe great praise for his creativity. These writings have taken on different meanings for different people. For some they are spiritual, for others a lesson in economics, politics, education and social development. Still others find the writings to be simply adventurous. The idea for the story came to Defoe from actual sailor accounts that were common at the time. Some say he stole the story from Alexander Selkirk, who spent five years alone on the island of Juan Fernandez. Others disagree with this, saying that Defoe wrote much more than a survival story. Some consider **Robinson Crusoe to be** autobiographical, claiming that Defoe may have hinted as much in mentioning his feeling of social isolation. He passed away on April 26, 1731, at the age of 71.*

"Heal the past; Live the present; Dream the future."

Anonymous

Strawberry Shortcakes

2 CUPS FLOUR
1/4 CUP SUGAR
3 TEASPOONS BAKING POWDER
½ TEASPOON SALT
½ CUP BUTTER
¾ CUP MILK
SWEETENED STRAWBERRIES
WHIPPED CREAM

HEAT OVEN TO 450 DEGREES. GREASE COOKIE SHEET. IN LARGE BOWL, COMBINE FLOUR, SUGAR, BAKING POWDER AND SALT. USING A PASTRY BLENDER, CUT IN THE BUTTER UNTIL THE MIXTURE HAS A CONSISTENCY OF COARSE MEAL. ADD MILK AND STIR JUST UNTIL THE DRY INGREDIENTS ARE MOISTENED. DROP THE DOUGH BY ROUNDED TABLESPOONS, APPROXIMATELY TWO INCHES APART, ONTO A GREASED COOKIE SHEET. BAKE FOR 10 TO 12 MINUTES OR UNTIL GOLDEN BROWN AND SERVE IMMEDIATELY.

CRUSH ABOUT ONE HALF OF THE STRAWBERRIES AND MIX THEM WITH THE REST OF THE WHOLE OR SLICED STRAWBERRIES. SPOON THE BERRIES OVER THE SHORTCAKES IN INDIVIDUAL BOWLS. TOP THE SHORTCAKES WITH WHIPPED CREAM AND GARNISH WITH WHOLE OR SLICED BERRIES. MAKES 8 SERVINGS.

ISLAND OF THE BLUE DOLPHINS

by

Scott O'Dell

"Summer is the best time on the Island of the Blue Dolphins. The sun is warm then and the winds blow milder out of the west, sometimes out of the south. It was during these days that the ship might return and now I spent most of my time on the rock, looking out from the high headland into the east, toward the country where my people had gone, across the sea that was never-ending. Once while I watched I saw a small object which I took to be the ship, but a stream of water rose from it and I knew that it was a whale spouting. During those summer days I saw nothing else. The first storm of winter ended my hopes. If the white men's ship were coming for me it would have come during the time of good weather. Now I would have to wait until winter was gone, maybe longer. The thought of being alone on the island while so many suns rose from the sea and went slowly back into the sea filled my heart with loneliness. I had not felt so lonely before because I was sure that the ship would return as Matasaip had said it would. Now my hopes were dead. Now I was really alone."

Discussion Questions

- *Did you trust Captain Orlov when he made the pact with Chief Chowig? If you were Chief Chowig, would you have agreed to the deal? Were you surprised by the outcome?*

- *How did you feel when Karana swam back to Ramo? Do you think you would have done the same thing if faced with a similar situation? Do you think if Karana had known that going back would mean 18 years alone on the island, she would have still done it?*

- *Did you trust Tutok when she first arrived on the island?*

- *What kind of impact did Karana's animal friends have on her, especially Rontu and Rontu-Aru?*

- *Do you feel differently about the book knowing that it is based on real events, rather than a fictional story?*

Interesting Facts

Scott O'Dell was born in Los Angeles in 1898. **Island of the Blue Dolphins** *is based on historical reports of an Indian girl who lived on San Nicolas Island off the coast of California from 1835 to 1853. O'Dell won the Newberry Medal for* **Island of the Blue Dolphins** *in 1961 and also won the Hans Christian Anderson Award for his body of work. The book was also named by the Children's Literature Association in 1976 as one of the ten best American children's books of the past 200 years. O'Dell wrote 26 books for children as well as fiction and non-fiction books for adults. He passed away in 1989 at the age of 91. His family was pleasantly surprised when upon his request, they went to scatter his ashes over the Pacific Ocean and found their boat being escorted by a dozen dolphins.*

"No matter where I serve my guests, it seems they like my kitchen best."

Anonymous

Strawberry Fruit Smoothie

10 OUNCES OF CRUSHED PINEAPPLE (INCLUDING JUICE)
1 BANANA
2 CUPS FRESH OR FROZEN STRAWBERRIES
3 CUPS OF ICE CUBES (USE CRUSHED ICE DEPENDING ON
BLENDER)
1/4 CUP MILK
½ CUP GRENADINE (STRAWBERRY SYRUP)

MIX ALL INGREDIENTS TOGETHER ON HIGH SPEED IN YOUR BLENDER. YOU MAY GARNISH
THE TOP OF THE CUP WITH A WHOLE STRAWBERRY OR A WEDGE OF PINEAPPLE.

THE EAGLE HAS LANDED
by

Jack Higgins

Prologue

"At precisely one o'clock on the morning of Saturday, November 6, 1943, Heinrich Himmler, Reichsfuhrer of the SS and Chief of State Police, received a simple message: "The Eagle has landed." It meant that a small force of German paratroopers were at that moment safely in England and poised to snatch the British Prime Minister, Winston Churchill, from the Norfolk country house where he was spending a quiet weekend near the sea. This book is an attempt to re-create the events surrounding that astonishing exploit. At least fifty percent of it is documented historical fact. The reader must decide for himself how much of the rest is a matter of speculation, or fiction."

Discussion Questions

- *What do you feel motivated Steiner to first accept the mission, and then to follow through after the mission encountered difficulties?*
- *Do you agree with Molly's contention (in reference to why she helped Liam and Steiner escape) that "love is a separate issue – it's in a compartment of its own?"*
- *What symbolism, if any, did you perceive in the fact that the German officers wore two uniforms? What impact do you feel this had on the people of Studley Constable, i.e., did they see the officers in two different ways? Name all of the characters who were subject to impersonations.*
- *What stereotypes did the local villagers have about the Germans? Were they correct? What stereotypes do you have about your "enemies" that may not withstand scrutiny? Why do people feel a need to vilify their adversaries?*
- *What portion of this book do you believe is based on actual events? Why?*

Interesting Facts

Henry "Harry" Patterson was born July 27, 1929 in Newcastle-on-Tyne, England, to Henry and Henrietta Higgins Patterson. He served in the British Army and in the Royal Horse Guard from 1947 to 1949. He received his teaching certificate from the Leeds Training Center in 1958. That same year, he married Amy Margaret Hewitt, and together they had four children: Sarah, Ruth, Sean, and Hannah. He later attended the London School of Economics and Political Science, and earned his Bachelor's Degree. When asked where he stands politically, he claims, "slightly right of center." Their marriage ended in 1984. In 1985, he married Denise Lesley Anne Palmer. Patterson began writing while he was a school master in England. He stated: "I was struggling very much to make some kind of living by writing, but I could not because the return on each book was so small. That meant that I had to publish books one after the other, so I used several names." He had an Irish uncle who was in the military that he admired, so he based his pseudonym, Jack Higgins, after his uncle. Patterson greatly enjoys writing about World War II, adding a mix of fact and fiction. He is best known for **The Eagle Has Landed.** *When asked how he views himself, Patterson answered, "I look upon myself primarily as an entertainer."*

*"We must laugh
We must sing
We are blest by everything!"*

Anonymous

Strawberry Pretzel Dessert

2 1/2 CUPS PRETZEL STICKS

1½ CUBES BUTTER

8 OUNCES CREAM CHEESE

1 CUP POWDERED SUGAR

2 CUPS WHIPPED TOPPING

1 LARGE PACKAGE STRAWBERRY GELATIN

2 CUPS FRESH OR FROZEN STRAWBERRIES

2 CUPS PINEAPPLE JUICE

1 CUP ICE CUBES FOR FRESH FRUIT OR

1 CUP COLD WATER FOR FROZEN FRUIT

MELT BUTTER IN 9 X 13 PAN AND STIR IN BROKEN PRETZEL STICKS. BAKE AT 400 DEGREES FOR TEN MINUTES. REMOVE FROM OVEN AND COOL COMPLETELY. POUR THE PINEAPPLE JUICE INTO A PAN AND BRING TO A BOIL. ADD GELATIN MIX AND STIR UNTIL DISSOLVED. ADD THE ICE CUBES AND FRUIT. IF USING FROZEN FRUIT, ADD 1 CUP OF COLD WATER INSTEAD OF ICE CUBES. PLACE THE MIXTURE IN THE REFRIGERATOR UNTIL THE GELATIN BEGINS TO SET.

MIX THE CREAM CHEESE AND SUGAR TOGETHER AND GENTLY FOLD INTO THE WHIPPED TOPPING. ONCE THE PRETZELS ARE COMPLETELY COOLED, GENTLY LAYER THE CREAM CHEESE MIXTURE OVER THE PRETZELS. AFTER THE GELATIN HAS BEGUN TO SET, GENTLY SPOON IT OVER THE CREAM CHEESE MIXTURE. REFRIGERATE UNTIL FIRMLY SET. WHEN READY TO SERVE, YOU MAY WANT TO TOP OFF EACH SERVING WITH A DOLLOP OF WHIPPED TOPPING, IF DESIRED

"The first of earthly blessings, Independence."

Edward Gibbon

June & July

LONG SUMMER BOOKS

As time went on and our reading competence grew, so did the length of some of our books. With inflated confidence, we attempted the nearly impossible task of having everyone in our book club finish a 1000-plus page book in one month while still maintaining our homes and families. Unwilling to admit failure and wanting another month to finish the book, we capitalized on the situation and started one of our most beloved book club traditions, the summer family barbecue! Now, instead of discussing only half of the book, we spend a book club evening getting to know each other's families and sharing a "pot luck" dinner in a park or backyard. When we meet the next month, we take great pride in having involved our families in something we love and in having finished a substantial book. Yes, these books are long ones, and are great reads.

The Brothers Karamazov

by

Fyodor Dostoyevsky

"We are all cruel, we are all monsters, we all make people weep, mothers and babies at the breast, but of all – let it be settled now once and for all – of all I am the most vile and despicable wretch! So be it! Every day of my life, beating my breast, I've vowed to turn over a new leaf, and every day I've done the same vile things. I realize now that such men as I, need a blow, a blow of fate, to catch them as though with a lasso and bind them by force from without. Never, never should I have risen of my own free will! But the lightning has struck. I accept the suffering of my accusation and of my public disgrace. I want to suffer and be cleansed by suffering! I will, perhaps, be cleansed, gentleman, won't I!"

Discussion Questions

- Discuss the personalities of the three brothers Karamazov: Dimitri, Ivan and Aloysha. Why are they so different?

- What influence did Zossima have on Aloysha's life? How did he use his influence to later impact the lives of other youth?

- What similarities do you see between Ivan and his story of the Grand Inquisitor?

- Who did you first think was responsible for Fyodor's ultimate downfall?

Interesting Facts

Fyodor Dostoevsky was born October 30, 1821 in Moscow, Russia, to Mikhail and Maria Dostoevsky. He was the second of seven children. His father was a physician at the hospital where Fyodor was born. He was a heavy drinker and not a very responsible father. His mother, on the other hand, was caring and loving to her children. The family lived at the Marinsky Hospital where his father worked. Fyodor's childhood was very confined, with no outside playmates, and he became very demanding and jealous.

When he was ten, his parents bought a farm outside of Moscow, which should have been a welcome improvement in Fyodor's life. Unfortunately, the new home continued to provide a sad life for the family. When Fyodor was fifteen, his mother grew ill and died. This was very difficult for him and he suffered from depression most of his life. Fyodor and one brother, Michael, were sent off to the Military Engineering Academy in St. Petersburg. Each new student was initiated by being whipped as they crawled on "all fours". Fyodor hated school, but did well with his studies.

Fyodor's father was murdered in 1839. This event haunted him, and when he started to write, the subjects of murder and crime were always present, and were the basis of later novels like **The Brothers Karamazov** and **Crime and Punishment**. Many of Dostoevsky's articles were politically controversial but he continued to publish them, even though they were illegal. He became known as a rebel writer and was sentenced to prison. He was later given a death sentence, and was supposed to be shot by a firing squad. The terrible scene was set, Dostoevsky was bound and blindfolded, with rifles aimed, when a messenger from the Czar arrived with a reprieve.

He was later sent to Siberia and lived under terrible conditions. This experience forced him to re-examine his life and he went through a spiritual reformation. When he left Siberia he continued to pursue his literary career. He had to publish novels at top speed to help pay for his substantial debt. By the end of his life he was debt free and was able to compose his last novel, **The Brothers Karamazov**, which was published in 1880. He died one year.

"Let Freedom Ring Everywhere!"

Anonymous

*Veggie Pizza**

8 OUNCE ROLL OF CRESCENT ROLL DOUGH
8 OUNCE CREAM CHEESE (SOFTENED)
1 ½ TEASPOONS MAYONNAISE
1 TABLESPOON DRY RANCH DRESSING MIX OR DILL WEED
SALT AND PEPPER TO TASTE

PREHEAT OVEN TO 350 DEGREES. SPREAD THE CRESCENT ROLL DOUGH OUT FLAT ONTO A PIZZA PAN OR BAKING STONE. PINCH ALL OF THE SEAMS TOGETHER. BAKE FOR 10-12 MINUTES, UNTIL LIGHTLY BROWNED. REMOVE FROM OVEN AND LET IT COOL COMPLETELY. BLEND TOGETHER THE REMAINING INGREDIENTS, AND SPREAD OVER THE COOLED CRUST.

GRATE ENOUGH CHEDDAR CHEESE TO COVER THE CREAM CHEESE MIXTURE, AND THEN SPRINKLE CHEESE OVER THE PIZZA. CHOP OR SLICE YOUR FAVORITE VEGETABLES AND SPRINKLE THEM OVER THE CHEESE. SOME CHOICES ARE:

CARROTS (GRATING IS EASIER THAN FINELY CHOPPING)
BROCCOLI
CAULIFLOWER
ZUCCHINI
MUSHROOMS
GREEN AND RED BELL PEPPERS
GREEN ONIONS
ROMA TOMATOES

YOU CAN CUT THE PIZZA IN WEDGES OR SQUARES TO SERVE.
*ADAPTED FROM THE PAMPERED CHEF RECIPE

Les Miserables

by

Victor Hugo

"The book which the reader now holds in his hands, from one end to the other, as whole and in its details, whatever gaps, exceptions, or weaknesses it may contain, treats of the advance from evil to good, from injustice to justice, from falsity to truth, from darkness to daylight, from blind appetite to conscience, from decay to life, from bestiality to duty, from Hell to Heaven, from limbo to God. Matter itself is the starting-point, and the point of arrival is the soul. Hydra at the beginning, an angel at the end."

Discussion Questions

- If faced with the same situation as Jean Valjean, in providing for his sisters' family, would you have stolen the bread? What impact did this one act of destitution have on the course of the rest of his life?

- How did Fantine's ultimate sacrifice for Cosette affect you? What did you think of the Thenardier family? Eponine? How about Javert? Do you feel he was inherently good or bad?

- Jean Valjean performed several unselfish and heroic acts. Which ones were your favorites? Why?

- How did you feel when Cosette and Marius turned away from Jean Valjean? Do you think Jean Valjean should have defended himself and confessed everything? Did the ending make you feel that your heart, like Jean Valjean's, would break?

Interesting Facts

Victor-Marie Hugo was born on February 26, 1802 in Besancon, France. He was a small baby and was not expected to live. His father was a high ranking officer in Napoleon's army and moved the family several times. Before Victor was two years old, his parents were separated and he spent the remainder of his childhood moving between parents around Napoleon's Empire. He was exiled in 1851 because of his opposition to Louis Napoleon. This made him a model of French resistance. He ended up on the Isle of Guernsey and it was there that he began to think more about **Les Miserables**. Hugo came down with anthrax and expected an early death. **Les Miserables** became his last chance to say everything that was in his heart. In 1861 he returned to Waterloo for the rest of his research.

After 30 years of thinking and working on **Les Miserables**, **Fantine** was published on April 3, 1862. The first part of the novel was so popular that people stood in line to get a copy and the book's characters became household names, long before the remaining sections were released. Much of **Les Miserables** was based on actual historical events, and experiences of real people, including Victor Hugo. There was a liberated convict named Pierre Maurin who turned to the door of Bishop Miollis after being rejected everywhere else. Marius parallels Victor in both love and politics. It was the human side of his character that appealed so greatly to the masses. Hugo was paraded through the streets as a national hero upon his return to Paris after the Revolution of 1870.

Les Miserables is just as popular today, and has engaged audiences all over the world, not only in print, but on the stage, and the big screen. The Tony Award winning musical has been seen by over 45 million people with a total gross of over $1.8 billion. There have been over 34,000 performances in 200 cities. Les Miserables became the second longest-running show in Broadway history on January 25, 2002.

More interesting facts on Victor Hugo can be found on page 104

"There is nothing like a dream to create the future."

Victor Hugo

Shrimp Cocktail Dip

4½ ounce can small shrimp
(rinsed, drained and coarsely chopped)
1 cup dairy sour cream
¼ cup chili sauce
2 teaspoons lemon juice
½ teaspoon prepared horseradish (may add more to taste)
¼ teaspoon seasoned salt
Dash of hot pepper sauce

In a small bowl, combine all ingredients. Cover and refrigerate for several hours or overnight to allow flavors to blend. Serve with crackers or baguette slices. Makes 1¾ cups.

DON QUIXOTE
by
Miguel de Cervantes

"Well, well!" exclaimed Sancho. 'So Lorenzo Corchuelo's daughter is the lady Dulcinea del Toboso, otherwise called Aldonza Lorenzo?' 'She is,' said Don Quixote, 'and she it is deserves to be mistress of all the world.' 'I know her well,' said Sancho, 'and I can tell you that she pitches a bar as well as the strongest lad in all the village. Praise be to God! She's a brawny girl, well built and tall and sturdy, and she will know how to keep her chin out of the mud with any knight errant who ever has her for his mistress. O the wretch, what muscles she's got, and what a pair of lungs! ... But I confess to you Don Quixote, that I have been very much mistaken on one point up to now. I really and truly thought that the lady Dulcinea must be some princess your worship was in love with, or at least a person of quality, to deserve the rich presents you sent her...' 'I have told you very often before now, Sancho,' said Don Quixote, 'that you are a very great babbler. Yet although your wits are blunt, your remarks sometimes sting ... I am quite satisfied, therefore, to imagine and believe that the good Aldonza Lorenzo is lovely and virtuous...and, for my part, I think of her as the greatest princess in the world.'"

Discussion Questions

- Do you consider Don Quixote a madman, or just a great actor? Explain?

- Don Quixote was a true optimist: he saw castles instead of inns. "[I]nstead of seeing two dowdy prostitutes, he sees ladies of quality who respond kindly to his courteous greetings." What can we learn about passing judgment from him?

- Discuss Sancho's character. Why do you think he was so faithful to Don Quixote?

- What were your favorite and most memorable "knight-errand" adventures?

Interesting Facts

Miguel de Cervantes was born in Alcala de Henares, in 1547, to Rodrigo and Leonor de Cervantes. He was the fourth of seven children. His father was a surgeon, and much of Miguel's childhood was spent moving from town to town, with his father trying to find work. In 1569 he moved to Italy and studied Italian literature and philosophy. He also fought in the battle of Lepanto in 1571, receiving a wound that permanently crippled his left arm. While returning to Spain, he was captured by pirates and sold as a slave. He was bought by the viceroy of Algiers, and attempted to escape many times. In 1580, his family finally raised 500 escudos, enough to purchase his freedom.

In 1584, he married Catalina de Salazar y Palacios, who was eighteen years younger than him. They did not have any children together, but Cervantes had a daughter, Isabel, from an affair with an actress, Ana de Villafranca. Isabel lived as a servant in the home of Cervantes' mother. He eventually left his wife, went bankrupt, and was imprisoned at least twice. When a nobleman was killed in front of Cervantes' home, Cervantes and the women in the house were jailed, suspected of committing the crime.

At the age of 58, Cervantes completed Part I of **Don Quixote.** It was his first big literary success. He completed Part II in 1614. His character, Don Quixote, has become the most famous figure in Spanish literature. It is rumored that even Shakespeare read Don Quixote. In spite of the fame that this novel brought him, Cervantes died in poverty on April 23, 1616.

Love not what you are, but what you can become.
Never stand begging for what you have the power to earn.

Miguel de Cervantes

Taco Bean Dip

On a large plate spread out the ingredients as follows:

Layer 1: 16 oz. can refried beans
Layer 2: 8 oz. sour cream mixed with one tablespoon of taco seasoning
Layer 3: 2 cups grated cheddar cheese
Layer 4: 3 green onions (thinly sliced)
Layer 5: 1 tomato (cubed)
Layer 6: ½ large can black olives (sliced)
Layer 7: 1 tablespoon chopped cilantro
(add a sprig of the cilantro to the center of the dip as a garnish)

Serve with restaurant style white corn tortilla chips.
Guacamole can be added as an additional layer.

VANITY FAIR
by
William Makepeace Thackeray

"All the world used her ill, said this young misanthropist, and we may be pretty certain that persons whom all the world treats ill, deserves entirely the treatment they get. The world is a looking-glass, and gives back to every man that reflection of his own face. Frown at it, and it will in turn look sourly upon you; laugh at it and with it, and it is a jolly kind companion; and so let all young persons take their choice."

Discussion Questions

- *Compare Rebecca's and Amelia's contrasting personalities.*

- *Discuss the differences between George Osborn and William Dobbin.*

- *Would you agree that the plot took a circular journey? Explain.*

- *Thackeray labeled this work as "a novel without a hero". Do you agree?*

- *Why do you think Lord Steyne continued to give Rebecca everything she requested, even after he discovered her true character?*

- *Discuss the differences in Georgy and Rawdy. Were you surprised by their personalities?*

Interesting Facts

*William Makepeace Thackeray was born in Calcutta, India in 1811. His family was wealthy, but because of bad luck, poor financial management and Thackeray's own squandering and compulsive gambling, the money was lost. Thackeray married an Irish girl named Isabella, whom he used as a model for Amelia. They had three daughters, the second of which died in infancy. Isabella fell claim to mental illness after the birth of their third child and was sent away to be cared for outside the family. The children lived with Thackeray's mother, while he struggled to earn a living submitting whatever he could to newspapers. Isabella never recovered. Thackeray went to Paris to study art, disappointing his mother who wanted him to study the law. He was a very talented caricaturist and he illustrated his own pictures for Vanity Fair as well as other books. After being rejected three or four times, **Vanity Fair** was finally published in 1847-1848 by Bradbury and Evans, Charles Dickens' publisher. It was published in serial form without time for Thackeray to make revisions where needed. As a result, time sequences are somewhat jumbled and character names are not always used consistently. Thackeray wrote to his mother concerning **Vanity Fair**, "My object is not to make a perfect character or anything like it. Don't you see how odious all the people are in the book (with the exception of Dobbin) behind whom all, there lies a dark moral, I hope. What I want is to make a set of people living without God in the world (only that is a "can't" phrase) greedy, pompous, mean, perfectly self-satisfied, for the most part and at ease about their superior virtue." Charlotte Bronte thought Thackeray to be a wonderful writer and dedicated her novel Jane Eyre to him.*

"Never lose a chance of saying a kind word."

William Makepeace Thackeray

Chocolate Chip Cheese Ball

8 OUNCE PACKAGE CREAM CHEESE (SOFTENED)
½ CUP BUTTER (NO SUBSTITUTIONS)
¼ TEASPOON VANILLA EXTRACT
2 TABLESPOONS BROWN SUGAR
¾ CUP POWDERED SUGAR
1 CUP MILK CHOCOLATE CHIPS (DIVIDED)
½ CUP DICED ALMONDS

IN A MIXING BOWL, COMBINE THE CREAM CHEESE, BUTTER AND VANILLA. MIX TOGETHER UNTIL FLUFFY. GRADUALLY ADD THE SUGARS, MIXING ONLY UNTIL THE SUGARS ARE COMBINED WITH MIXTURE.

USING A CHEF'S KNIFE, CHOP ¾ OF THE CHOCOLATE CHIPS INTO VERY SMALL PIECES. CAREFULLY FOLD THE SMALL PIECES INTO THE CREAM CHEESE MIXTURE. COVER AND CHILL FOR ABOUT TWO HOURS.

TOAST THE ALMONDS FOR 5 TO 10 MINUTES ON A BAKING SHEET, IN AN OVEN PREHEATED TO 375 DEGREES. STIR ALMONDS OFTEN WHILE ROASTING. PLACE THE REMAINING CHOCOLATE CHIPS IN A BLENDER OR FOOD PROCESSOR AND CHOP INTO A FINE POWDER. MIX THE FINE POWDER WITH THE ALMONDS.

AFTER THE CREAM CHEESE MIXTURE HAS COOLED FOR TWO HOURS, REMOVE IT FROM THE REFRIGERATOR. PLACE THE MIXTURE IN PLASTIC WRAP OR WAX PAPER AND FORM INTO A BALL. SET BALL AND WRAPPING INSIDE OF A BOWL AND CHILL FOR AT LEAST ONE ADDITIONAL HOUR. IMMEDIATELY PRIOR TO SERVING, REMOVE THE PLASTIC WRAP AND ROLL THE BALL IN THE ALMOND AND CHOCOLATE MIXTURE. SERVE THE CHEESE BALL WITH A VARIETY OF HONEY, CINNAMON, AND/OR CHOCOLATE GRAHAM CRACKERS.

"My life is like a stroll upon
the beach, as near to the
ocean's edge as I can go."

Henry David Thoreau

August
VACATION BOOKS

Vacations are supposed to be fun and enjoyable despite the hassle of travel. Reading a good book is often the perfect way to pass the time during a long airport layover, boat, train or car ride. Even after our destination has been reached, some of us love nothing more than to kick back and read while laying in the sun, relaxing in the hotel room, or while hanging out in a tent. Vacation books, however, must meet certain criteria. They must be relatively easy to read, contain short chapters, and be entertaining enough to hold our attention. After all, noone should have to work too hard at having fun!

THE POISONWOOD BIBLE
by
Barbara Kingsolver

"'Tata Jesus is Bangala!' declared the Reverend every Sunday at the end of his sermon. More and more, mistrusting his interpreters, he tries to speak in Kikongo. He throws back his head and shouts these words to the sky, while his lambs sit scratching themselves in wonder. Bangala means something precious and dear. But the way he pronounces it, it means the poisonwood tree. Praise the Lord, hallelujah, my friends! for Jesus will make you itch like nobody's business."

Discussion Questions

• Did you like the way the author used the four daughters, Rachel, Leah, Adah and Ruth to tell the majority of their life's journey? Did you enjoy any one storytelling style over the others? Which one and why?

• Each sister had a unique personality and experience in the Congo. Did you relate to one of the sisters more than the others? Who would you most likely have acted like if you had been asked to fulfill this same missionary service at a young age?

• Discuss your feelings toward the Reverend Price? What were your feelings for Orleanna Price?

• Share your favorite part of the book. What did you glean from the story?

Interesting Facts

Barbara Kingsolver was born on April 8, 1955 in Annapolis, Maryland to Dr. Wendell and Virginia Henry Kingsolver. She attended DePauw University, and graduated magna cum laude in 1977. She continued her graduate work at the University of Arizona, and received her Master's Degree in 1981. In 1985 she married Joseph Hoffman, who worked as a chemist, and together they had a daughter, Camille. The couple later divorced. She is now married to Steven Hopp, with whom she has a daughter, Lily. Barbara enjoys music, hiking, gardening and parenthood. She has received many awards for her writing, including The "Book Sense" Book of the Year Award in 2000 for **The Poisonwood Bible**. Barbara personally spent time in the Congo where this book was set, which gave her great inspiration for the best seller. It spent 30 weeks on the best sellers list for hardbacks and another 36 weeks on the paperback best seller's list. The New York Times called this novel, "a powerful book . . . ." The Chicago Tribune wrote, "Kingsolver is such an extraordinary storyteller." Oprah Winfrey also chose **Poisonwood** for one of her book club selections. Kingsolver has not only contributed through her literary works, but also as a human rights activist. She established and funds the Bellwether Prize, an endowment that awards $25,000 biannually, and guarantees the publication of a first time author of a novel addressing social injustice and the impact of culture and politics on human relationships. Kingsolver describes herself as "a writer of the working class." "My idea of a prewriting ritual is getting the kids on the bus and sitting down."

"Leisure is being allowed to do nothing."

G.K. Chesterton

Chips and Fresh Salsa

Fresh Salsa

5 large tomatoes, peeled and cubed (pour off excess juice)

1/3 cup chopped onion (Walla Wallas are preferred)

1 small green pepper, chopped

2 green onions, sliced

1/4 teaspoon crushed garlic

1 lime, juiced

1 tablespoon sugar

1 teaspoon salt

a few shakes of Tabasco

2 tablespoons of fresh cilantro (add more to taste)

Mango Salsa

2 ripe mangos, peeled and cubed

1 large tomato, peeled and cubed

½ cup minced onion

1 large red bell pepper

2 tbs. chopped fresh cilantro (or more to taste)

1 tablespoon chili pepper or a couple dashes of Tabasco

1 lime, juiced

1 tablespoon sugar

1 teaspoon salt

Mix all of the above ingredients together and serve with restaurant-style white corn tortilla chips.

ALL CREATURES GREAT AND SMALL

by

James Herriot

"Mrs. Pumphrey was an elderly widow. Her late husband, a beer baron whose breweries and pubs were scattered widely over the broad bosom of Yorkshire, had left her a vast fortune and a beautiful house on the outskirts of Darrowby. Here she lived with a large staff of servants, a gardener, a chauffer and Tricki Woo. Tricki Woo was a Pekingese and the apple of his mistress' eye . . . Siegfried's face was expressionless as he read the card aloud. `Tricki requests the pleasure of Uncle Herriot's company on Friday, February 5th. Drinks and dancing.' He looked up and spoke seriously. `Now isn't that nice? You know, that must be one of the most generous Pekingese in England. Sending you kippers and tomatoes and hampers isn't enough-he has to ask you to his home for a party.' I grabbed the card and slipped it out of sight. `All right, all right, I know. But what am I supposed to do?' `Do? What you do is to sit right away and get a letter off saying thank you very much, you'll be there on February the fifth. Mrs. Pumphrey's parties are famous. Mountains of exotic food, rivers of champagne. Don't miss it whatever you do.' `Will there be a lot of people there?' I asked, shuffling my feet. Siegfried struck himself on the forehead with his open hand. `Of course there will be a lot of people. What d'you think? Did you expect it would be just you and Tricki? You'd have a few beers together and then you'd dance a slow foxtrot with him? The cream of the county will be there in full regalia but my guess is that there will be no more honoured guest than Uncle Herriot. Why? Because Mrs. Pumphrey invited the others but Tricki invited you."

Discussion Questions

• Discuss some of your most memorable "house calls" made by Dr. Herriott.

• What did you think of Mrs. Pumphrey and her animals, especially her beloved dog, Tricki Woo?

• Discuss the relationships between James and Siegfried and James and Tristan. What did you like and dislike about the men?

• Did knowing that reading this book was like reading Dr. Herriott's journal make it more interesting for you? Do you think his wife, Joan, enjoyed reading about their courtship in this book? How would you feel if there was a similar book about your life?

Interesting Facts

James Alfred Wight was born on October 3, 1916 in Sutherland, County Tyne and Wear, England, to James Henry and Hannah Bell Wight. His father was a musician and his mother was a professional singer. When he was thirteen years old, he read a magazine article about the life of a veterinarian, "and that did it, nothing could shake [his] determination to train as an animal vet". He attended the Glasgow Veterinary College and graduated in 1938. He went to work that same year for a Dr. Sinclair, a country vet in Thirsk, Yorkshire, England. He was later made a partner and the office name was changed to Sinclair & Wight. He fell in love with Joan Catherine Danbury and they married on November 5, 1941. They had two children, a son, named after his father, and a daughter, Rosemary. James Sr. was quoted as saying, "The life of a country vet was dirty, uncomfortable, sometimes dangerous. It was terrible hard work and I loved it. I felt vaguely that I ought to write about it and everyday for 25 years I told my wife about something funny that had happened and said I was keeping it for a book. She usually said 'yes, dear' to humor me but one day, when I was 50, she said: 'Who are you kidding? Vets of 50 don't write first books.' Well, that did it. I stormed out and bought some paper and taught myself to write." He elaborated further, "It's against the ethics of the veterinary profession to advertise and when I first started writing my books, I was afraid some of my peers might think it unprofessional to write under my own name. So I was sitting in front of the T.V. tapping out one of my stories and there was this fellow James Herriot playing such a good game of soccer for Birmingham that I just took his name." After four years of learning to write and enduring publishers' rejections, his first book, **If Only They Could Talk** was published in 1970 in England. It only sold 1,200 copies. His next book was, **It Shouldn't Happen To A Vet.** An American publisher picked it up, combined the two books as one named, **All Creatures Great and Small -- which became an instant bestseller**. This success was the start of an incredible writing career that launched a series of books, including **All Things Bright and Beautiful, All Things Wise and Wonderful, The Lord God Made Them All** and **Every Living Thing.** His writings are too numerous to count, and include many children's books. In 1974 **All Creatures Great and Small** was made into a movie, starring Anthony Hopkins and Simon Ward. Herriott enjoyed visiting the filming location, which was close to his home. He continued working at his office, Sinclair & Wight, until 1992. He was diagnosed with prostate cancer and died February 23, 1995 in Thirsk, Yorshire, England.

"We must never be afraid to go too far, for success lies just beyond."

Marcel Proust

Frozen Fruit Cocktail

5 CUPS FRESH PEACHES (SLICED)
I CUP SUGAR
¼ CUP LEMON JUICE (MIXED WITH ¼ CUP WATER)
¾ CUP ORANGE JUICE
20 OUNCE CAN CRUSHED PINEAPPLE (DO NOT DRAIN)

COMBINE ALL OF THE ABOVE INGREDIENTS AND FREEZE COMPLETELY. (BEST TO FREEZE OVERNIGHT IF POSSIBLE.) ONE HOUR PRIOR TO SERVING, REMOVE INGREDIENTS FROM FREEZER AND DEFROST. IN A BOWL, SMASH THE PARTIALLY FROZEN MIXTURE WITH A POTATO MASHER UNTIL IT IS BROKEN UP.

THEN STIR IN:
2 SMALL BANANAS (MASHED)
2-3 CUPS OF ORANGE SHERBET
I-3 CUPS LEMON-LIME SODA

AFTER STIRRING IN BANANAS AND SHERBET, POUR IN LEMON-LIME SODA I CUP AT A TIME, CONTINUING TO ADD MORE SODA AND STIR UNTIL THE DESIRED CONSISTENCY IS ACHEIVED. SERVE IN A GOBLET OR STEMMED GLASS.

DIVINE SECRETS OF THE YA-YA SISTERHOOD

by

Rebecca Wells

"To Ya-Ya-rabilia," Caro said, raising her cup in a toast. "What?" Vive asked. "Life is short, Pal," Caro said. "Send the scrapbook." "It is not my fault if she's chickening out of her wedding," Vivi said. "I am not sending her my scrapbook." "I'm the godmother," Caro said. "Send the 'Divine Secrets.'" "It would be the well-mannered thing to do," Necie said. "Send the 'Divine Secrets,' cher," Teensy said. "Send it tout de suite." Vivi looked at each of her friends. Finally, she raised her glass. "To Ya-Ya-rabilia," Vivi said, and raised her glass. Then, each of them in turn met each other's eyes as they clinked glasses. This is a cardinal Ya-Ya rule: you must meet each person's eyes while clinking glasses in a toast. Otherwise, the ritual has no meaning, it's just pure show. And that is something the Ya-Ya's are not.

Discussion Questions

• *What were your feelings about Vivi as a mother? What were your feelings about Vivi's mother? Do you believe Vivi and her mother had a cause and effect relationship?*

• *In your opinion, who is the heroine of the book? Why?*

• *What good or bad influence did the Ya-Ya's have on each other? What influence have your friends had in your life?*

• *List the attributes of a good friend.*

• *What does "knowing how to love" mean to you?*

Interesting Facts

Rebecca Wells was born in central Louisiana and has always had a soft spot in her heart for the South. After traveling and studying acting throughout the United States, she chose to make her home in the Pacific Northwest. She began writing and staging plays at an early age and eventually wrote, **"Splittin' Hairs",** *which has toured in 50 states. Her play,* **"Gloria Duplex",** *was also well received. After achieving success as both an actor and play write, she began writing a novel in her mid thirties.* **"Little Alters Everywhere"** *became Rebecca's first novel about the "Ya-Yas" and was followed by* **"The Divine Secrets of the Ya-Ya Sisterhood."** *When asked if the books were autobiographical, Rebecca says the stories are fiction, the product of good story telling. Early success of the two books came mostly from word of mouth.* **"Divine Secrets of the Ya-Ya Sisterhood"** *has now become a major motion picture and has brought "Ya-Ya" groups to life all over the country. Rebecca Wells says, "What I'm finding is that somehow the books seem to bring out girl groups. And I use the word "girl" lovingly. I'm not going to say women's groups, because I think when women get together like this, it brings out the part that is girl, and that is a good, good part." Fans will be happy to know that after the book version of* **"Splittin' Hairs"** *is complete, they can expect to see a third "Ya-Ya" book.*

"It is the sweet, simple things in life which are the real ones after all."

Laura Ingalls Wilder

Chocolate Cream Pie

Pie crust:

¼ CUP WATER
1/2 CUP BUTTER FLAVORED SHORTENING
1/2 TEASPOON SALT
1 CUP FLOUR

QUICKLY MIX ALL OF THE INGREDIENTS TOGETHER IN THE ORDER SHOWN ABOVE UNTIL JUST BLENDED. DO NOT OVERWORK THE DOUGH; THE LESS IT IS HANDLED, THE FLAKIER IT WILL BE. ROLL OUT THE PASTRY ON A FLOURED SURFACE AND PLACE IN AN UNGREASED PIE PAN. POKE THE BOTTOM AND SIDES OF DOUGH WITH A FORK GENEROUSLY TO PREVENT BUBBLING. BAKE THE CRUST AT 350 DEGREES FOR 10-20 MINUTES. DEPENDING ON THE THICKNESS OF THE CRUST, REMOVE WHEN CRUST IS FIRM, BEFORE IT TURNS BROWN. POKE DOWN ANY ADDITIONAL BUBBLES THAT MAY DEVELOP DURING BAKING. REMOVE FROM THE OVEN AND LET COOL.

Chocolate Filling:

1 LARGE PACKAGE INSTANT CHOCOLATE PUDDING
12 OUNCE CONTAINER OF WHIPPED TOPPING
MILK CHOCOLATE CANDY BAR (4 OUNCE)

FOLLOW THE DIRECTIONS ON THE BOX FOR THE INSTANT PIE FILLING. FOLD ONE CUP OF THE WHIPPED TOPPING INTO THE PUDDING AND THEN POUR MIXTURE INTO THE PIE SHELL. COVER PUDDING WITH REMAINING WHIPPED TOPPING. GRATE THE CHOCOLATE BAR WITH CHEESE CUTTER OR GRATER AND SPRINKLE THE SHAVINGS OVER THE WHIPPED TOPPING. REFRIGERATE FOR SEVERAL HOURS BEFORE SERVING.

CHARMS FOR THE EASY LIFE

by

Kaye Gibbons

"She asked me whether she was normal or abnormal. She wasn't abnormal. That word described the old man who roamed about downtown, grabbing people by the sleeve, telling them the time, temperature, and current world news that had no connection to reality. Or the little girl we had just read about in the paper who wasn't sure of her age or name but could do fantastically long sums in her head. They were abnormal. My grandmother was certainly nothing like these two, but she wasn't normal in the sense of being like other people who worked in banks or stores, women with permanent waves and moisturized skin. But all the same, in the strangest sort of way, I considered her normal for herself. It was normal for her to eat two cloves of raw garlic every morning, wear her late mother's seventy-five year old shoes, preserve the laces in linseed oil, and sit up all night laughing uproariously over Tristram Shandy. I thought of all these things, and more, and said, 'Well, you're not what I would call abnormal, but you have done some things people might call odd.' 'Yes, this is true,' she said. 'I have picked up a habit or two along the way. If I hadn't, I'd bore myself into the grave in about two days.'"

Discussion Questions

• *What did you find endearing about Grandma Charlie Kate? Do you think she is completely nuts?*
• *How did you feel about the relationship of the grandmother, mother and granddaughter? Was there anything that you envied about them?*

• *What was the most memorable "house call"? Why?*

• *What do you foresee for Sophia and Margaret and their relationships with Mr. Richard Baines and Tom Hawkings III?*

Interesting Facts

*Kaye Gibbons was born in Nash County, North Carolina in 1960. She attended Rocky Mountain High School, and then continued her education at the University of North Carolina at Chapel Hill. While studying American Literature at the University, she wrote and published her first novel, **Ellen Foster**. **Charms for the Easy Life** was her fourth novel. It was published in 1993 and was on the New York Times Bestseller List. Time magazine stated, "Some people might give up their second-born to write as well as Kaye Gibbons." She was also the youngest writer to ever receive the Chevalier de L'Ordre des Arts et des Lettres, a French knighthood recognizing her contribution to French literature. Her other titles include **Ellen Foster, A Virtuous Woman** (which was chosen by Oprah Winfrey as one of her Book Club selections), **A Cure for Dreams, Sights Unseen** and **On the Occasion of My Last Afternoon**. She has been the recipient of many awards, including the Sue Kaufman Award for First Fiction from the Academy of Arts and Letters, the 1990/PEN Revson Award for the best work of fiction published by a writer under the age of 35. She has also received The Heartland Prize for Fiction from The Chicago Times, the Sir Walter Raleigh Award, a special citation from the Ernest Hemingway Foundation, and the Louis Rubin Writing Award from the University of North Carolina, as well as their Distinguished Alumnus Award. Hallmark Hall of Fame also made **Ellen Foster** into a movie which aired on CBS television. Kaye and her family reside in North Carolina.*

"The mind is like a parachute; it works best when it is open."

Anonymous

Fresh Peach Dessert

Layer #1

2 ½ CUPS GRAHAM CRACKERS (CRUSHED)
½ CUBE BUTTER (MELTED)
6 TABLESPOONS POWDERED SUGAR

COMBINE THE ABOVE INGREDIENTS AND TAKE OUT 1/4 CUP OF THE CRUMBS. PRESS THE REMAINING CRUMBS IN THE BOTTOM OF A 9 X 13 PAN. THE REMAINING CRUMBS WILL BE USED ON THE TOP OF THE DESSERT.

Layer #2

2 CUPS WATER
1/2 CUP SUGAR
2 TABLESPOONS CORN STARCH
1 LARGE PACKAGE PEACH GELATIN
5 CUPS FRESH SLICED PEACHES

COMBINE THE WATER, SUGAR AND CORN STARCH IN A PAN. BRING TO A BOIL, AND CONTINUE BOILING UNTIL MIXTURE BECOMES THICK. REMOVE FROM THE HEAT AND ADD THE PACKAGE OF GELATIN. PLACE IN REFRIGERATOR UNTIL IT COOLS COMPLETELY AND STARTS TO THICKEN. WHEN THE GELATIN MIXTURE IS READY, REMOVE FROM REFRIGERATOR AND STIR IN THE FRESH PEACHES. POUR OVER THE TOP OF THE GRAHAM CRACKER CRUMBS. REFRIGERATE FOR ABOUT ONE HOUR UNTIL IT IS SET.

Layer #3

8 OUNCES CREAM CHEESE
½ CUP POWDERED SUGAR
12 OUNCE CONTAINER OF WHIPPED TOPPING

BEAT TOGETHER THE CREAM CHEESE AND POWDERED SUGAR. FOLD IN WHIPPED TOPPING AND SPREAD OVER THE PEACHES. SPRINKLE THE REMAINING GRAHAM CRACKER CRUMBS OVER THE TOP. REFRIGERATE FOR SEVERAL HOURS, UNTIL GELATIN IS COMPLETELY SET.

*"Who takes the child by
the hand takes the
mother by the heart."*

Sans-serif German Proverb

September

KID'S FAVORITES

The words "back to school" have a way of bringing out the child in all of us. The books featured in this section have proven enjoyable to both young and old alike. You will never regret passing on your own love of books, or spending time reading with you children, grandchildren, nieces, nephews, or young neighbors and friends. (Maybe you will regret it a little when you find your children reading instead of doing their chores.) But don't be too hard on them, we still do the same thing as adults.

HARRY POTTER AND THE SORCERERS STONE

by

J. K. Rowling

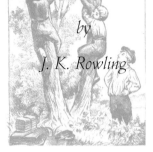

"...it matters not what someone is born, but what they grow to be!"

Discussion Questions

• *What character or event surprised you the most? What parts of the story were you able to predict? What are your predictions for future Harry Potter books?*

• *The author, J.K. Rowling, patterned the bookish and bossy Hermione after herself. What character in the book do you identify with the most? What character do you most admire?*

• *If you were a professor at Hogwarts, what subject would you most enjoy teaching? (i.e., Potions, Spells, Herbology, Transfiguration, History of Magic, Defense against the Dark Arts, Quidditch, Divination, Care of Magical Creatures, etc.) Why?*

• *There has been a lot controversy surrounding the Harry Potter series. Some people believe the books should be banned from schools because they encourage and promote witchcraft and favor the occult. What is your opinion?*

Interesting Facts

J. K. Rowling was born in 1965 and wrote her first book when she was six years old. It was a book about a rabbit and was appropriately titled, **Rabbit**. *She loved reading the book Little White Horse when she was young and especially loved the way the author described the horse's diet in so much detail. This book greatly influenced her own writing style, including her invention of "Bertie Bott's Every Flavor Beans." As a single mother trying to make a living as a teacher, Ms. Rowling struggled to do the best she could. She found she could only get her daughter to sleep if she was moving, so she would walk Jessica to the nearest pub, where she would write as Jessica slept. When asked how she was able to do it all, she said, "I didn't do housework for four years and I lived in squalor . . . I can't do everything."* **Harry Potter and the Philosopher's Stone** *was rejected by several publishing companies before being picked up by Bloomburg for approximately $4,000. J. K. Rowling says that nothing since has felt greater than the first moment she knew that she was finally going to be published. The book did well in England, but Rowling was still primarily making her living as a teacher. All that changed when America caught wind of the book in 1997 and Scholastic offered her $105,000 for the book rights, an unprecedented amount for a first time author. By 1999 Rowling had become an international superstar with the first three Harry Potter books appearing on the New York Times Bestsellers list, all at the same time. The film,* **Harry Potter and the Sorcerer's Stone** *was released in November 2001 with the biggest movie opening ever. Rowling says of her success, "the reality of it has been strange and terrible at times." Rowling wishes she could share her success with her mother who died of multiple sclerosis at the age of 45. She has drawn on the experiences of losing her mother when relating the loss of Harry's parents, especially the scene in the book when he stumbles upon the mirror of Erised. She says she knows all too well the thought, "Please, God, just give me five more minutes." In response to the criticism that her books are too dark and full of witchcraft, Rowling states she does not believe in or practice witchcraft. She made up all of the ideas in the books, taking great liberties with ideas that she borrowed from folklore. She says, "People underestimate children, they know it is fiction."*

"Self-confidence is the first requisite to great undertakings."
                                                              Samuel Johnson

Peanut Butter Rice Crispies

1 CUP SUGAR

1 CUP LIGHT CORN SYRUP

1 CUP PEANUT BUTTER (CREAMY OR CHUNKY)

1 TEASPOON VANILLA OR RUM EXTRACT

1/2 TEASPOON CINNAMON

1/2 PACKAGE CHOCOLATE CHIPS

1/2 PACKAGE BUTTERSCOTCH CHIPS

6 CUPS RICE CRISPIES CEREAL

IN A SMALL SAUCEPAN, ADD THE SUGAR AND CORN SYRUP TOGETHER. HEAT UNTIL THE SUGAR MELTS AND THE SYRUP BEGINS TO BUBBLE. DO NOT LET LIQUID COME TO A BOIL. TAKE THE PAN OFF THE STOVE. ADD THE PEANUT BUTTER, VANILLA/RUM EXTRACT AND CINNAMON. STIR TOGETHER UNTIL ALL INGREDIENTS ARE THOROUGHLY MIXED. MIX IN THE CEREAL. LIGHTLY GREASE OR SPRAY A 9 X 3 PAN AND POUR IN CONTENTS. MIX THE CHOCOLATE AND BUTTERSCOTCH CHIPS IN A MICROWAVABLE BOWL AND MELT IN THE MICROWAVE FOR ONE MINUTE. STIR CONTENTS AND RETURN TO MICROWAVE FOR ONE ADDITIONAL MINUTE. REPEAT UNTIL CHIPS ARE MELTED. ONCE CHIPS ARE COMPLETELY MELTED, STIR AGAIN AND POUR THE MELTED CHIPS OVER THE CONTENTS IN PAN. LET STAND FOR SEVERAL HOURS TO ALLOW THE CHOCOLATE TO SET UP. (OPTIONAL: PLACE ONE COLORFUL PEANUT M&M ON TOP OF EACH SQUARE).

THE CHRONICLES OF NARNIA

by

C.S. Lewis

In Narnia the Beasts lived in great peace and joy and neither the Witch nor any other enemy came to trouble that pleasant land for many hundred years. King Frank and Queen Helen and their children lived happily in Narnia and their second son became King of Archenland. The boys married nymphs and the girls married wood-gods and river-gods. The lamppost which the Witch had planted (without knowing it) shone day and night in the Narnian forest, so the place where it grew came to be called the Lantern Waste; and when, many years later, another child from our world got into Narnia, on a snowy night, she found the light still burning. And that adventure was, in a way, connected with the ones I have just been telling you.

Discussion Questions

• *Why do you think that Queen Jadis lost her strength when she, Digory and Polly were in the Woods between the Worlds? Why did she regain her strength when she got to London (or our world)?*

• *Why do you think C.S. Lewis chose a lion for Aslan's character?*

• *Discuss some of the similarities between the creation period of Narnia and the biblical creation, found in Genesis in the Bible.*

• *How did you feel about the warning that Aslan gave to Digory and Polly in the last chapter about the immediate state and future of our world? How do you feel about his comparison of our world with the world of Charn?*

Interesting Facts

When C.S. Lewis was seven years old, his family moved into a large house named "Little Lea." It was full of rooms, stairways and passages. One of the rooms had a large oak wardrobe made by Lewis' grandfather. Lewis would sit in the wardrobe with his older brother, Warnie, and tell him stories. It was common in 1939 for children living in London to be sent to the country for safety. Some of these "evacuees" came to live with Lewis while he was caring for the mother of one of his friends who was killed in the war. One of the evacuees asked Lewis if there was anything behind the wardrobe. This question got Lewis started on the idea for **The Chronicles of Narnia***. At first, there really was no story, just pictures in his head. He began writing it in 1950. Lewis gave the story to his friend, J. R. R. Tolkien, who was very critical of the story. Tolkien felt Lewis had written the story too quickly, without giving it the same time and energy that Tolkien had given his own stories.*

A little boy sent a letter asking Lewis in which order **The Chronicles of Narnia** *should be read. The boy suggested reading them in this order:* **The Magician's Nephew, The Lion, the Witch, and the Wardrobe, The Horse and his Boy, Prince Caspian, The Voyage of the Dawn Treader, The Silver Chair,** *and* **The Last Battle***. Lewis agreed with the boy, even though his suggestion was not the order in which the books were published. The* **Chronicles of Narnia** *have appeared as stage plays, radio shows, television shows, cartoon films and have been recorded with several famous actors and actresses. C. S. Lewis died on November 22, 1963, but his death went largely unnoticed as John F. Kennedy was assassinated on the same day.*

*More interesting facts of C. S. Lewis can be found on page 16.

"The aim of education is the knowledge not of facts, but of values"

Dean William Ralph Inge

Miniature Banana Muffins

½ CUP SHORTENING

½ CUP SUGAR

2 EGGS, BEATEN

1 ½ CUP MASHED BANANAS OR APPLESAUCE

½ TEASPOON CINNAMON

½ TEASPOON BAKING SODA

1 TEASPOON BAKING POWDER

½ TEASPOON SALT

2 CUPS FLOUR

CHOPPED WALNUTS, OPTIONAL

CINNAMON CHIPS, OPTIONAL

CREAM SHORTENING AND SUGAR, THEN ADD THE REMAINING INGREDIENTS. IF YOU DON'T HAVE ENOUGH BANANAS YOU CAN MAKE UP THE DIFFERENCE WITH APPLESAUCE. SPOON BATTER INTO MINIATURE MUFFIN TINS. FILL EACH CUP TO THE TOP WITH BATTER THAN SPRINKLE ON NUTS OR CINNAMON CHIPS, IF DESIRED. BAKE AT 350 DEGREES FOR 15 MINUTES OR UNTIL TOOTHPICK COMES OUT CLEAN.

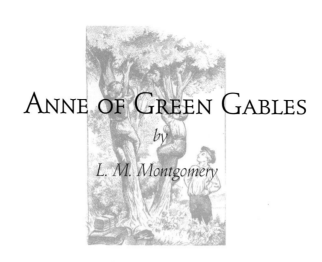

Anne of Green Gables

by

L. M. Montgomery

"You don't want me!" she cried. "You don't want me because I'm not a boy! I might have known it was all too beautiful to last. I might have known nobody really did want me. Oh, what shall I do? I'm going to burst into tears!" Burst into tears she did. Sitting down on a chair by the table, flinging her arms out upon it, and burying her face in them, she proceeded to cry stormily. Marilla and Matthew looked at each other deprecatingly across the stove. Neither of them knew what to say or do. Finally Marilla stepped lamely into the breach. "Well, well, there's no need to cry so about it." "Yes, there is need!" The child raised her head quickly, revealing a tear stained face and trembling lips. "You would cry, too, if you were an orphan and had come to a place you thought was going to be home and found that they didn't want you because your weren't a boy. Oh, this is the most tragical thing that ever happened to me!"

Discussion Questions

• *Mathew, Marilla and Anne would be considered an unconventional family. How would the situation be different today? Would the family be more acceptable today?*

• *What were your initial feelings about Mathew and Marilla taking in an orphan? What were your feelings when they told Anne she could not stay? What would you have done in the same situation?*

• *The community had varied responses to Anne. Some were hesitant while others were very accepting. Do you feel some people were quick to judge, or were they just being cautious? Were their responses justified? What are your feelings about children achieving success when placed in a positive, encouraging environment?*

• *Of Anne's many mishaps, which is your favorite? Why? What did you learn from Anne?*

Interesting Facts

*Lucy Maud Montgomery was born November 30, 1874 in Canada's smallest province, Clifton. Her mother died of tuberculosis when Lucy was 21 months old and she was left to live with her grandparents. Her father kept in touch and finally sent for her when she was fifteen. Lucy had always loved books, writing and school work. She started writing in a journal when she was nine and continued to write in it for the next 60 years. Lucy always dreamed of being a writer and began writing **Anne of Green Gables** in secret, as she greatly feared being mocked if the book was a failure. Her idea for the book was inspired when a neighbor adopted a girl from an orphanage, but it was several years before she began to write. The book was finished within a few months and was sent to and rejected by five publishers. The completed work sat in a closet for a year before she circulated it again. **Anne of Green Gables** was published on June 10, 1908 by L.C. Page Company in Boston. It was a huge success with 37 editions published in six years in several languages. The book was written for girls, but was just as popular among adults, including soldiers, trappers and missionaries abroad. The story of Anne Shirley has been made into movies, plays, television shows and cartoons. The home Lucy used as a model for Green Gables and the Lucy Maud Montgomery Museum are visited by over 100,000 tourists each year. In 1911, Lucy wrote the following of Anne in her journal, "Does she not stand at my elbow even now – if I turned my head quickly should I not see her – with her eager, starry eyes and her long braids of long hair and her pointed chin? To tell that haunting elf that she is not real because, forsooth, I never met her in the flesh. No, I cannot do it. She is so real that, although I've never met her, I feel quite sure I shall some day . . ."*

"Children have more need of models than of critics"
Joseph Joubert

Jell-O Pudding Poke Cake

1 CAKE MIX (WHITE, YELLOW OR LEMON)
1 SMALL PACKAGE JELL-O (FLAVOR OF YOUR CHOICE)
1 SMALL PACKAGE INSTANT PUDDING (FLAVOR OF YOUR CHOICE)
2 CUPS WHIPPED TOPPING (THAWED)

FOLLOW THE CAKE DIRECTIONS ON BOX AND BAKE IN A 9 X 13 CAKE PAN. COOL THE CAKE FOR 15 MINUTES. WITH A DINNER FORK, POKE LINES OF HOLES ACROSS THE CAKE (APPROXIMATELY 40 POKES) PREPARE JELL-O AS DIRECTED AND SPOON IT OVER CAKE. LET THE CAKE COOL COMPLETELY. PREPARE THE PUDDING AS DIRECTED ON THE BOX AND THEN FOLD IN THE WHIPPED TOPPING. SPREAD THE TOPPING OVER THE TOP OF THE CAKE. REFRIGERATE FOR SEVERAL HOURS, UNTIL IT IS READY TO SERVE. SINCE THERE ARE ENDLESS VARIATIONS, HERE ARE SOME:

LEMON CAKE/ORANGE JELL-O/LEMON PUDDING
WHITE CAKE/PINEAPPLE JELL-O/COCONUT CREAM PUDDING
BABY SHOWER: WHITE CAKE/BLUE OR PINK JELL-O/WHITE CHOCOLATE OR VANILLA PUDDING
CAKE SHOWN: WHITE CAKE/RASPBERRY JELL-O/CHEESECAKE PUDDING

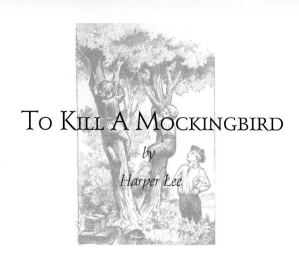

TO KILL A MOCKINGBIRD

by

Harper Lee

"When he gave us our air-rifles, Atticus wouldn't teach us to shoot. Uncle Jack instructed us in the rudiments thereof; he said Atticus wasn't interested in guns. Atticus said to Jem one day, "I'd rather you shot at tin cans in the back yard, but I know you'll go after birds. Shoot all the blue jays you want, if you can hit 'em, but remember it's a sin to kill a mockingbird." That was the only time I ever heard Atticus say it was a sin to do something, and I asked Miss Maudie about it. "Your father's right," she said. Mockingbirds don't do one thing but make music for us to enjoy. They don't eat up people's gardens, don't nest in corncribs, they don't do one thing but sing their hearts out for us. That's why it's a sin to kill a mockingbird."

Discussion Questions

- *How did you feel about Atticus Finch as a man, and as a single father?*
- *What were some of the pros and cons you encountered with Scout as the narrator of the story?*
- *When did you realize what type of a person Boo Radley was?*
- *Imagine yourself living in Maycomb in the 1930's; how do you think you would have handled the controversial situations?*
Would you have befriended any of the characters? Would you have made any enemies?

Interesting Facts

Harper Lee ("Nelle") was born on April 28, 1926 in Monroeville, Alabama. She is the daughter of Amasa Coleman and Frances Finch Lee, and a descendent of General Robert E. Lee. Like her character, Scout, Harper's father was a lawyer. She attended Huntington College for one year and then went to the University of Alabama and graduated in 1949. She also attended Oxford University. After graduation, while finishing her legal studies, she began her writing career.

*She started writing short stories while working to support herself as an airline reservation clerk. A literary agent encouraged her to turn the stories into a novel, so she quite her job to work full time on the project. After several years and with the help of good friends who believed in her work, **To Kill A Mockingbird** was published. It was an immediate success, winning the Pulitzer Prize in 1961 as well as several other awards. It continues today to be a favorite assignment in high school and college courses. Lee claims that the book is not autobiographical, but it is does draw upon her own childhood experiences of being raised in a small southern town. Her older sister, Sook, like Boo Radley, was a recluse and rarely left their home. She and Boo share many of the same characteristics. **To Kill A Mockingbird** is Lee's only novel, yet she is a leading figure in American literature. Many have praised her work, including Edgar H. Schuster, who states, ". . . she has placed race prejudice in a perspective which allows us to see it as an aspect of a larger thing; as something that arises from phantom contacts, from fear and lack of knowledge; and finally as something that disappears with the kind of knowledge or 'education' that one gains through learning what people are really like when you 'finally see them.'" Harper Lee enjoys traveling and lives in her hometown of Monroeville, Alabama.*

"It is not attention that the child is seeking but love."

Sigmund Freud

Spudnuts

1 CUP SCALDED MILK

½ CUP SUGAR

1/4 CUP SHORTENING

1 TEASPOON SALT

3/4 CUP MASHED OR INSTANT POTATOES

2 EGGS

1/4 TEASPOON NUTMEG

4 CUPS FLOUR

1/4 CUP WARM WATER

1 TABLESPOON YEAST

IN A MIXING BOWL, COMBINE THE FIRST FIVE INGREDIENTS. SOFTEN THE YEAST IN THE WARM WATER. ADD YEAST TO THE MILK MIXTURE. BEAT IN EGGS, NUTMEG AND FLOUR. LET THE DOUGH RISE UNTIL IT DOUBLES IN SIZE. ON A LIGHTLY FLOURED SURFACE, ROLL OUT THE DOUGH UNTIL IT IS 1 ½ INCHES THICK. CUT OUT DOUGHNUTS AND LET THEM RISE FOR 1 HOUR. FRY IN HOT OIL (AROUND 400 DEGREES) TURNING ONCE, UNTIL GOLDEN BROWN. GLAZE DOUGHNUTS WHILE THEY ARE STILL HOT WITH:

3 CUPS POWDERED SUGAR

½ CUP WATER

1 TEASPOON VANILLA

"Autumn makes a demand...
that we learn to let go -
to acknowledge the beauty of sparseness."
                    Bonaro W. Overstreet

October

SCARY BOOKS

October is known for bringing out the monsters, vampires, and phantoms.
These stories offer a look from whence these spooks have come.
Those easily frightened might read them during the day,
While those slightly squeamish might have to look away.
As autumn leaves blow and jack-o-lanterns burn bright,
You're sure to be scared by these books on Halloween night!

DRACULA
by
Bram Stoker

"The window at which I stood was tall and deep, stone-mullioned, and though weatherworn, was still complete; but it was evidently many a day since the case had been there. I drew back behind the stonework, and looked carefully out. What I saw was the Count's head coming out from the window. I did not see the face, but I knew the man by the neck and the movement of his back and arms. In any case I could not mistake the hands which I had had so many opportunities of studying. I was at first interested and somewhat amused, for it is wonderful how small a matter will interest and amuse a man when he is a prisoner. But my very feelings changed to repulsion and terror when I say the whole man slowly emerge from the window and begin to crawl down the castle wall over that dreadful abyss, face down with his cloak spreading out around him like great wings. At first I could not believe my eyes. I thought it was some trick of the moonlight, some weird effect of shadow; but I kept looking, and it could be no delusion. I saw the fingers and toes grasp the corners of the stones, worn clear of the mortar by the stress of years, and by thus using every projection and inequality move downwards with considerable speed, just as a lizard moves along a wall. What manner of man is this, or what manner of creature is it in the semblance of man? I feel the dread of this horrible place overpowering me; I am in fear-awful fear-and there is no escape for me; I am encompassed about with terrors that I dare not think of ..."

Discussion Questions

- *First off, were you "scared to death" while reading this book? What parts did you find the most frightening?*
- *Did you enjoy the way the author used journal entries and letters to tell so much of the story? Why?*
- *Count Dracula appeared in many different forms. Discuss his appearances and the situations that surrounded them.*
- *Discuss Renfield's character and his purpose in the storyline.*

Interesting Facts

Abraham "Bram" Stoker was born on November 8, 1847 in Clontarf, Ireland, just north of Dublin. His father, Abraham was a civil servant and his mother, Charlotte was a social activist. He was the third of seven children. Bram was a very sickly child and was often bedridden during his first seven years. To entertain him, his mother would make up gruesome tales, which became one of Bram's favorite pastimes. His father also had an incredible library and Bram spent many hours reading. When he was still a child he started making up and writing his own ghost stories, and told friends and family that he would someday be famous for his writing.
He attended Trinity College in Dublin, and graduated in 1870. He received honors in math and excelled in athletics. After college he, like is father, worked as a civil servant, but did not enjoy the work, for his real love was writing.

*On December 4, 1878, he married Florence Anne Lemon Balcombe, and together they had one child, Noel. In 1882 Stoker received a medal from the Royal Humane Society, for talking a stranger out of committing suicide. He later attended Middle Temple University in London and studied law. He was admitted to the bar in 1890. Stoker worked as the manager at the Lyceum Theatre in London, where he and his wife enjoyed the social life that accompanied his position. He was honored to meet Arminius Vambery, a Hungarian adventurer and professor, who told wonderful stories of vampires in Eastern Europe. Stoker was so intrigued that he started doing his own research. He conducted four years of in-depth research on the subject. His research, together with a terrible vampire nightmare that came to him one night after an indulgent crab dinner, resulted his novel, **Dracula**, which brought him lasting fame. Stoker helped establish the vampire as one of the most recognizable figures in the modern arts. His story has been adapted for film, television, stage, recordings and comic books. Stoker died of syphilis on April 20, 1912, in London, England.*

"The dearest ones of time, the strongest friends of the soul-Books."
Emily Dickinson

Caramel Apple Dip

8 OUNCE CREAM CHEESE
¾ CUP BROWN SUGAR
½ CUP POWDERED SUGAR
¾ CUP TOFFEE BITS (FOUND NEAR THE CHOCOLATE CHIPS AT THE GROCERY STORE)
I TEASPOON VANILLA

THOROUGHLY MIX THE ABOVE INGREDIENTS, AND PLACE IN A SERVING BOWL. SERVE WITH A NICE VARIETY OF SLICED APPLES. (MAKE SURE TO SLICE YOUR APPLES INTO A BOWL OF WATER WITH "FRUIT FRESH" OR LEMON JUICE ADDED TO KEEP THEM NICE AND WHITE.)

FRANKENSTEIN
by
Mary Shelley

"I am malicious because I am miserable. Am I not shunned and hated by all mankind? You, my creator, would tear me to pieces, and triumph; remember that, and tell me why I should pity man more than he pities me? You would not call it murder if you could precipitate me into one of those ice-rifts, and destroy my frame, the work of your own hands. Shall I respect man when he condemns me? Let him live with me in the interchange of kindness; and, instead of injury, I would bestow every benefit upon him with tears of gratitude at his acceptance. But that cannot be; the human senses are insurmountable barriers to our union. Yet mine shall not be the submission of abject slavery. I will revenge my injuries: if I cannot inspire love, I will cause fear; and chiefly towards you my arch-enemy, because my creator, do I swear inextinguishable hatred. Have a care: I will work at your destruction, nor finish until I desolate your heart, so that you shall curse the hour of your birth."

Discussion Questions

• For whom did you feel more sympathy; Victor Frankenstein or his creation?

• How believable was the scenario of the creature learning to do everything by watching the De Lacey family through a crack in the wall? How did you feel when the creature finally gained the courage to visit the family to thank them?

• Do you think that it would have been better if Frankenstein would have completed the companion for his creature? Do you think that the creature would have kept his promise?

• What do you think happened to the creature at the end of the story? Do you think he did as he said he would do?

Interesting Facts

Mary Wollstonecraft Godwin was born in August, 1797, in London. Her mother, a well known feminist, died a few weeks after Mary was born. She was raised by her father, an activist for the underprivileged, and by his second wife. Mary's father started a publishing company out of their home, where Mary met Percy Bysshe Shelley and his wife, Harriet. Mary and Percy eloped three months shy of her seventeenth birthday, accompanied by Mary's step sister Jane (Claire). Percy continued to see Harriet who was pregnant with their third child. In Percy's absence, Mary began having an affair with a man who was of great help to her after the death of Mary and Percy's premature daughter. Percy was comfortable with the affair, having himself become involved with Jane.

In 1816, Mary, Percy, their second child, William, and Jane moved close to Lake Geneva. Jane had an affair with poet Lord Byron, who lived nearby. They all spent time together at Byron's villa challenging one another to write ghost stories. It was in this atmosphere that the idea for **Frankenstein** was born. The book's publishing was substantially delayed due to Mary's move back to London, ill health during her third pregnancy, the suicide death of Mary's half sister, Fanny (who had always thought Mary had everything, including Percy), the suicide death of Harriet, who was also pregnant, and Mary's wedding to Percy. The book was published January 1, 1818. Mary's third child, Clara, died on September 24, 1818 from a tooth infection. Her son, William, died on June 7, 1819, of malaria while Mary was pregnant with her fourth child. Mary suffered a miscarriage in June 1821, and lost Percy in a drowning accident on July 8, 1822. Some say she carried Percy's heart in her purse until her own death in February 1851, at the age of 54.

"Adventure is not outside man; it is within."
David Grayson

Nutty Marshmallow Popcorn

16 CUPS POPPED POPCORN
1 CUBE BUTTER
1 1/3 CUPS SUGAR
½ CUP LIGHT CORN SYRUP
1 TEASPOON VANILLA
3 CUPS MINIATURE MARSHMALLOWS
2 CUPS MIXED NUTS

MIX THE POPCORN AND NUTS AND SET ASIDE. BRING BUTTER, SUGAR AND CORN SYRUP TO A BOIL, THEN TURN THE HEAT DOWN AND LET IT BOIL SOFTLY FOR THREE MINUTES. STIR CONSTANTLY. REMOVE FROM THE HEAT AND ADD MARSHMALLOWS AND VANILLA. POUR OVER POPCORN AND NUTS AND MIX WELL. SPREAD OUT ON WAXED PAPER AND LET COOL.

THE STRANGE CASE OF DR. JEKYLL AND MR. HYDE

by

Robert Lewis Stevenson

I must have stared upon it for near half a minute, sunk as I was in the the mere stupidity of wonder, before terror woke up in my breast as sudden and startling as the crash of symbols; and bounding from my bed, I rushed to the mirror. At the sight that met my eyes, my blood was changed into something exquisitely thin and icy. Yes, I had gone to bed Henry Jekyll, I had awakened Edward Hyde. How was this to be explained? I asked myself; and then, with another bound of terror–how was it to be remedied?

Discussion Questions

• *Do you believe as Dr. Jekyll did, that every person has a good side and an evil side?*

• *In the beginning of the story Dr. Jekyll was in control of Mr. Hyde. Discuss the transfer of power that occurred as the story unfolded.*

• *Which scene in the book did you find to be the most disturbing?*

• *What impact did Dr. Jekyll's guilt have on his personality, character and actions?*

Interesting Facts

Robert Louis Stevenson was born November 13, 1850 in Edinburgh, Scotland. He was the only child of Thomas and Margaret Isabella Stevenson. He was born an invalid with weak lungs, a trait he inherited from his mother. When he was six years old, he won his first award for his writing and was published at the age of sixteen. Robert's parents were very religious and his early writings depicted that influence. When he went away to college, however, his life style changed dramatically. He was known for his outrageous clothes and behavior and was nicknamed, "Velvet Jack." He was also involved with drugs, alcohol and women. By the age of 22, he claimed to be agnostic, which crushed his parents. He went on to study law and passed the bar in 1875, but never practiced. He loved writing and claims to have imitated some of his favorite writers, including Daniel Defoe.

When Stevenson was 26 he met an American women, eleven years his senior, Fanny Van de Grift Osbourne. The two met while Stevenson was trying to recuperate from a respiratory illness in France. They fell in love and dated for two years, but Fanny was already married with two children of her own. She eventually returned to her home and family in California.

*The following year he received a mysterious cable from Fanny and left immediately for America. With his poor health, the journey almost killed him. He then had to travel from New York to California. He joined an emigrant train, but almost lost his life several times along the way. When he was finally reunited with Fanny he was starving, incredibly sick, and penniless. His reward came when Fanny divorced her husband and they were married on May 19, 1880. In 1881, with the financial help of Robert's father, Robert, Fanny and her eleven year old son, Lloyd, returned to Scotland. During a rainy school holiday, Robert and Lloyd passed the time by drawing pictures. Robert drew an elaborate map of an island, he started telling a story to go with the map, and soon **Treasure Island** was created. **Kidnapped** was another one of his big hits. One night, Fanny awoke Robert from a terrible dream, he was screaming in his sleep. He was angry at her for waking him. "I was dreaming a fine bogey tale," he said. It was about a man who changed into a monster by a concoction made with white powder. He started writing furiously in bed the next morning. After three days he had completed 40,000 words of **The Strange Case of Dr. Jekyll and Mr. Hyde**. He proudly read the story to Fanny and Lloyd, but Fanny didn't like it. They got into a terrible argument and Robert threw the manuscript into the fire. Three days later he had rewritten the story, which brought him more success than he had ever known. Robert was very talented, and published several works, plays and media adaptations. He returned to his Christian beliefs in his later life. He died of a cerebral hemorrhage on December 3, 1894, at the age of 44.*

"Too much of a good thing is wonderful."

Mae West

Orange Bow Knots

Dry Yeast (1 package, cake or tablespoon)
¼ cup warm water
(add a teaspoon of sugar to help feed the yeast)
1 cup milk (scalded)
½ cup shortening
1/3 cup sugar
1 teaspoon salt
5-5 ½ cups flour
2 eggs (beaten)
2 tablespoons grated orange zest (outer peel)
1/4 cup orange juice

Soften the dry yeast in warm sugar water, and let sit for about ten minutes. Combine the milk, shortening, sugar and salt then let it cool to lukewarm. When lukewarm, stir two cups of flour into the milk mixture and beat well. Add the eggs and mix again. Stir in the softened yeast, 2 tablespoons of the orange peel, orange juice and then the remaining flour, enough to make a soft dough. Cover and let it rest for ten minutes.

Knead the dough for 8-10 minutes on a lightly floured surface until the dough is smooth and elastic. Place in a lightly greased bowl, turning once to grease the surface. Cover and let it rise for two hours. Punch down dough and let it rise again for ten minutes. Roll dough into a large rectangle and cut into half inch strips, ten inches long, and three-fourths of an inch wide. Lightly flour your fingers, then roll the strip of dough like a snake and loosely tie into a knot and pinch the ends together in the center. Place on a lightly greased cookie sheet, making sure to tuck in the pinched ends, so that you cannot see them. Bake at 375 degrees for 15 minutes or until done. While rolls are still warm, drizzle them with the orange icing.

Orange Icing:
1 tablespoons grated orange zest (outer peel)
3 tablespoons orange juice
1½ cups powdered sugar

The Phantom of the Opera
by
Gaston Leroux

"Such a little thing really, a kiss ... most people don't give it a moment's consideration. They kiss on meeting, they kiss on parting, that simple touching of flesh that is taken entirely for granted as a basic human right. I've lived on this earth half a century without knowing what it is to be kissed ... and I'll never know now."

Discussion Questions

• *Did you despise or pity Erik? Why?*

• *Discuss the differences between Christine Daae and Raoul de Chagny's relationship and Erik's relationship with Christine. Who do you feel loved Christine the most? Explain.*

• *What was the scariest part of the book? Which of Erik's traps and tricks did you find the most ingenious?*

• *What was Erik's greatest sacrifice for Christine?*

Interesting Facts

Gaston Louis Alfred was born May 6, 1868. His parents were returning from Le Mans to their home in Normandy, and had to change trains in Paris. Moving from one station to another was a tedious journey across the city for Marie-Alphonsine, who was nine months pregnant at the time. Labor pain began and she was rushed into a nearby home where she gave birth to Gaston. When he was older he returned to Paris to find the home where he was born. Upon learning that it had been purchased by an undertaker, he joked, "There, where I sought a cradle, I found a coffin." He attended school in Normandy, and then went to Paris where he graduated from law school. His parents were quite wealthy, and after his father's death, he inherited nearly one million francs. Within six months, he had lost all of his inheritance to drinking and gambling. He started working as a full-time journalist for a local newspaper. Investigative writing became his forte. He was quoted as saying, "No one can equal the reporter's zest for life, since nobody else possesses such a delight in observation. The reporter watches on the world's behalf, he is the spy-glass of the world. Oh, how I love my profession!" But in 1907, he gave it up to become a full-time novelist.

*Leroux wrote several novels and developed his plot lines from what he had learned from his major literary influences: Stendal, Alexandre Dumas and Victor Hugo. He wrote **The Mystery King**, which had a Monte Cristo theme, as a tribute to Dumas. In 1911 he wrote **The Phantom of the Opera**, it surprisingly received little attention in its first weeks. He was inspired to write the story after visiting the Paris opera house and became fascinated with the network of catacombs over which it was built. The labyrinth cellars and subterranean lake were once the holding cell for prisoners, where there was no chance of seeing the light of day. He also remembered the unfortunate accident in 1896 when one the chandeliers fell into audience. He wrote this story with such precision that the line between truth and imagination is almost invisible. He died on April 15, 1927, having lived long enough to enjoy the fame of the newly released film, **The Phantom of the Opera**. His death at 59 was brought on by complications from an acute urinary tract infection. He was buried in the Castle Cemetery, set high above Nice, overlooking the golden city and the azure Bay of Angels.*

"The writer is an explorer. Every step is an advance into a new land."

Ralph Waldo Emerson

Cinnamon Rolls

1 CUP SCALDED MILK

½ CUP BUTTER

½ CUP SUGAR

1 TEASPOON SALT

1 TEASPOON ALMOND FLAVORING

2 TABLESPOONS YEAST

½ CUP WARM WATER + 1 TABLESPOON SUGAR

2 EGGS

5 TO 5 ½ CUPS SIFTED FLOUR

COMBINE THE FIRST FIVE INGREDIENTS IN A LARGE BOWL. SOFTEN THE YEAST IN THE SUGAR WATER FOR ABOUT TEN MINUTES, THEN ADD TO THE MILK MIXTURE. MIX IN THE EGGS, AND THEN GRADUALLY STIR IN THE FLOUR. KNEAD AND POUND DOUGH FOR SEVERAL MINUTES, UNTIL THE DOUGH IS SMOOTH AND ELASTIC. PLACE DOUGH IN A BIG BOWL THAT HAS BEEN GREASED WITH COOKING OIL, TURNING ONCE TO GREASE THE TOP OF THE DOUGH. LET THE DOUGH RISE UNTIL IT DOUBLES IN SIZE, THEN PUNCH IT DOWN. (IF YOU HAVE TIME, YOU CAN LET THE DOUGH RISE A SECOND TIME.) ROLL OUT DOUGH INTO A RECTANGLE AND COVER VERY GENEROUSLY WITH:

½ CUP MELTED BUTTER

2 CUPS BROWN SUGAR

2 TABLESPOONS CINNAMON

NUTS (OPTIONAL)

RAISINS (OPTIONAL)

CHOCOLATE CHIPS (OPTIONAL)

START AT THE SHORT END OF THE RECTANGLE AND ROLL UP THE DOUGH. CUT WITH A KNIFE OR PIECE OF SEWING THREAD FOR CINNAMON ROLLS. ALTERNATIVELY, YOU CAN CUT THE RECTANGLE IN HALF LENGTHWISE AND FORM TWO SEPARATE TEA RINGS . PLACE EACH ROLL ON THE GREASED COOKIE SHEET. LET RISE UNTIL DOUBLE IN SIZE, AROUND 45 MINUTES. BAKE AT 350 DEGREES FOR 15 MINUTES UNTIL GOLDEN BROWN. (BAKE TEA RINGS FOR 25 MINUTES) WHILE ROLLS ARE STILL A LITTLE WARM, FROST WITH THE FOLLOWING:

Cream Cheese Frosting:

4 OZ. CREAM CHEESE

½ CUBE BUTTER

1 TEASPOON VANILLA OR ALMOND EXTRACT

4 CUPS POWDERED SUGAR

2-4 Tablespoons milk

BEAT TOGETHER WELL, ON LOW SPEED, UNTIL FLUFFY. THIN WITH MILK FOR DRIZZLING ON THE TEA RING.

*"For what I have received
may the Lord make me truly
thankful. And more truly for
what I have not received."*

Storm Jameson

November
INTERNATIONAL CLASSICS

November is often associated with gratitude and Thanksgiving. We want to express our gratitude to the authors of the world who have enlightened, enthralled and entertained us for so long. Thank you! Our lives would not be the same without them. Please keep the books coming!

THINGS FALL APART
by
Chinua Achebe

"The white man is very clever. He came quietly and peaceable with his religion. We were amused at his foolishness and allowed him to stay. Now he has won our brothers, and our clan can no longer act like one. He has put a knife on the things that held us together and we have fallen apart."

Discussion Questions

• *Discuss Okonkwo's character, especially his involvement in the devastating scene with Ikemefuna. How was this scene a turning point in the story?*

• *What explanation could you give, if any, for the tribal custom of dealing with twins? What Western traditions do we have in our society that other cultures many find strange?*

• *Obierika states that the white Christian missionaries have "put a knife on the things that held us together and we have fallen apart." What are some of the advantages and disadvantages that you saw as the missionaries converted more and more of the Igbo natives?*

• *How did you feel about the way that Igbo women were treated by their husbands and the community?*

• *What do you think was going through Okonkwo's mind as he "fell apart" at the end of the story?*

Interesting Facts

*Chinua Achebe (pronounced Chee-noo-ah Ah-chay-bay) was born November 16, 1930, in the Igbo town of Ogidi, Nigeria, to Isaiah Okafor and Janet Iloegbunam Achebe. He was the fifth of six children. At that time, Nigeria was under British rule and his parents named him Albert, after Prince Albert. It was in college that he changed to his Igbo name, Chinua, short for Chinualumogo, meaning, "My spirit come fight for me." He attended school at the same Christian church where his father was a teacher. His father retired when Chinua was five and the family moved back to their ancestral village of Ogidi, into a home of dirt wall and a tin roof. He started learning English at the age of eight. He became somewhat of a hero in his village, and was nicknamed "dictionary" for his knowledge of the English language. He married Christiana Chinwe Okoli in 1961, the same year that he became the first director of external broadcasting in Nigeria for the BBC. Together they had two sons and two daughters: Chinelo, Ikechukwu, Chidi and Nwando. Achebe's first novel, **Things Fall Apart**, was published in 1958. It was a huge success and won for the author many awards, including the Margaret Wong Memorial Prize. Achebe has been named by critics as the finest Nigerian novelist, as well as being placed among the best English language novelists from any country. In 1966, he was forced to move to eastern Nigeria because of the countryside persecution of the Igbo. He took an active part in their struggle for independence. He later became the director of African Studies at the University of Nigeria, and has also lectured extensively at many American universities. His novel, Things Fall Apart, is a literary classic and is read everywhere in the English-speaking world. It has been translated into at least 45 different languages, and has sold several million copies.*

"All the things of the universe are perfect miracles, each as profound as any."

Walt Whitman

*Frosty Pumpkin Dessert**

32 GINGERSNAPS (FINELY CRUSHED)
¼ CUP BUTTER (MELTED)

MIX TOGETHER AND PRESS IN A SPRINGFORM PAN, AND PLACE PAN IN THE FREEZER.

½ CONTAINER VANILLA ICE CREAM (SOFTENED)
2/3 CUP TOFFEE BITS
1 CUP WHIPPED TOPPING

MIX ABOVE INGREDIENTS TOGETHER AND POUR OVER THE CRUMBS AND RETURN TO THE FREEZER FOR ONE HOUR.

1 CUP PUMPKIN
1/3 CUP BROWN SUGAR
1½ TEASPOON PUMPKIN PIE SPICE
½ CONTAINER VANILLA ICE CREAM
1½ CUPS WHIPPED TOPPING

MIX ABOVE INGREDIENTS TOGETHER AND SPREAD OVER THE SECOND LAYER. RETURN TO THE FREEZER OVER
NIGHT, OR UNTIL COMPLETELY FROZEN. TAKE OUT OF THE FREEZER AND PLACE IN THE REFRIGERATOR AT LEAST
20 MINUTES BEFORE YOU WANT TO SERVE THIS YUMMY DESSERT. THIS WILL MAKE IT EASIER TO CUT. YOU MAY
WANT TO ADD A DOLLOP OF WHIPPED TOPPING WHEN READY TO SERVE.
*FROM THE PAMPERED CHEF

THE HUNCHBACK OF NOTRE DAME

by

Victor Hugo

"Suddenly, just as the executioner's assistants were about to carry out their orders, he climbed over the balustrade of the gallery and clutched the rope with his hands, knees and feet. The crowd saw him slide down the façade like a raindrop on a windowpane, run over to the executioner's assistants with the swiftness of a cat, fell them both with his enormous fists, take the gypsy girl in one arm as easily as a child picking up a doll and rush into the church, holding her above his head and shouting in a formidable voice, 'Sanctuary!' "

Discussion Questions

• Is it right to break the law when breaking the law means some people will benefit and some people will lose?

• What characters changed during the story and how did they change?

• Did you perceive any symbolism from the cathedral or the bells in the story? What did they symbolize?

• What human qualities did Quasimodo represent to you?

• What lessons did the book teach you about humans overcoming their imperfections? Do you believe that individuals can transcend their own nature to achieve spiritual greatness? Do you think that all people have some beautiful and grotesque characteristics like Quasimodo?

Interesting Facts

Victor Hugo was born prematurely and as a result suffered some physical limitations. As a young child his head appeared much to large for his small body. His head often flopped to one side and at times he looked like he had a hunched back. He spent a lot of time watching his older brothers play, unable to join them. Hugo first became known for his writing after submitting a poem in a contest sponsored by the Academie Francaise at the age of fifteen. He was later elected to the Academie. **The Hunchback of Notre Dame** was Hugo's first full length novel. It appeared in book shops on March 16, 1831. Hugo used to visit the cathedral of Notre Dame and explore wherever he could. He often climbed the bell towers and sat and looked over the city. He claimed to have discovered the word "fate" carved on a wall in a small room. Thus the story of **The Hunchback of Notre Dame** was born. By the 1840's, the success of The Hunchback had made Notre Dame a huge tourist attraction, complete with tour guides showing the carved message on the wall. Eventually, so many messages had been carved that no one could tell which was the original. Victor Hugo makes reference in The Hunchback to Nicolas Flamel, and his philosopher's stone. The stone has since been made famous by a story about a boy named Harry Potter. Hugo died in 1885. His body was put to rest in the Pantheon, one of Hugo's least favorite buildings. To him, it looked like a giant sponge cake. He was buried with honor having revolutionized French literature.

More interesting facts on Victor Hugo can be found on page 64

"The supreme happiness in life is the conviction that we are loved."

Victor Hugo

Pumpkin Roll

3 EGGS
1 CUP SUGAR
2/3 CUP CANNED PUMPKIN
1 TEASPOON LEMON JUICE
¾ CUP FLOUR
1 TEASPOON BAKING POWDER
2 TEASPOON CINNAMON
1 TEASPOON GINGER
½ TEASPOON NUTMEG
½ TEASPOON SALT
1 CUP CHOPPED WALNUTS (OPTIONAL)

SPRAY A JELLY ROLL PAN WITH NON-STICK SPRAY, LINE WITH WAXED PAPER, AND THEN SPRAY AGAIN. BEAT EGGS AND SUGAR UNTIL THICK, AND THEN ADD PUMPKIN AND LEMON JUICE. COMBINE THE DRY INGREDIENTS SEPARATELY, THEN ADD THEM TO THE PUMPKIN MIXTURE. POUR IN PAN AND SPRINKLE WITH WALNUTS IF SO DESIRED. BAKE AT 350 DEGREES FOR 15 MINUTES. THE SIDES OF THE CAKE WILL BEGIN TO PULL AWAY FROM THE PAN WHEN IT IS DONE. REMOVE CAKE FROM OVEN. LIGHTLY DAMPEN A CLEAN LINT-FREE KITCHEN TOWEL (FLOUR SACK TYPE). LAY IT ON THE COUNTER, AND THEN TURN THE HOT CAKE OVER ONTO THE TOWEL. NOW GENTLY ROLL UP THE TOWEL AND THE CAKE EITHER LENGTH WISE TO SERVE MORE PEOPLE, OR FROM THE END FOR A FATTER CAKE ROLL. LET COOL COMPLETELY.

Filling

8 OUNCE CREAM CHEESE (ROOM TEMPERATURE)
4 TABLESPOON BUTTER (ROOM TEMPERATURE)
1 CUP POWDERED SUGAR
1 TEASPOON VANILLA
2 CUPS WHIPPED TOPPING.

COMBINE TOGETHER THE CREAM CHEESE, BUTTER, POWDERED SUGAR, AND VANILLA WITH A HAND MIXER, AND THEN FOLD IN THE WHIPPED TOPPING. GENTLY UNROLL THE CAKE AND EVENLY SPREAD THE FILLING OVER THE CAKE. GENTLY ROLL IT BACK UP (WITHOUT THE TOWEL THIS TIME). PLACE ON A PLATTER AND COVER. REFRIGERATE UNTIL READY TO SERVE. IF YOU DID NOT ADD NUTS, YOU MAY WANT TO SPRINKLE SOME POWDERED SUGAR, THROUGH A SIFTER, ON TOP OF THE ROLL, IMMEDIATELY BEFORE SERVING. THIS RECIPE CAN BE MADE IN ADVANCE AND FROZEN FOR UP TO 30 DAYS.

THE RED BADGE OF COURAGE

by
Stephen Crane

"I've knet yeh eight pair of socks, Henry, and I've put in all yer best shirts, because I want my boy to be jest as warm and comf'able as anybody in the army. Whenever they get holes in 'em, I want yeh to send'em rightaway back to me, so's I kin dern'em. An allus be careful an' choose yer comp'ny. There's lots of bad men in the army, Henry. The army makes 'em wild, and they like nothing better than the job of leading off a young feller like you, as ain't never been away from home much and has allus had a mother, an' a-learning 'em to drink and swear. Keep clear of them folks, Henry. I don't want yeh to ever do anything, Henry, that yeh would be 'shamed to let me know about. Jest think as if I was a-watch'in yeh. If yeh keep that in yer mind allus, I guess yeh'll come out about right."

Discussion Questions

• *Do you think that Henry's search for self identity and courage were successful? Explain.*

• *Crane writes in a very impressionistic and symbolic manner (i.e. calling Henry just a small cog in the army). What were some of the other instances of this type of writing style that you noticed?*

• *There are two different stories in this book, what are they and how do they relate to each other? Why do you think Crane entitled this book,* **"The Red Badge of Courage"***?*

• *How did you feel about Henry Fleming's mother? What did she add to the story? What was the best piece of advice that she gave to her son?*

Interesting Facts

Stephen Crane was born in Newark, New Jersey, on November 1, 1871. Although he was born six years after the Civil War had ended, his most famous work, **The Red Badge of Courage,** *depicted the Civil War in dramatic detail. He was the fourteenth child in his family. His father, Dr. Jonathon Townley Crane, was a Methodist minister, as was his grandfather, and several other relatives on both sides of his family. At the age of three, Stephen taught himself to read and write, and regularly wrote letters to his grandmother. At the age of four he was reading novels. He had his first newspaper story published at the age of fifteen. His first novel was published at the age of 22, and his second,* **The Red Badge of Courage**, *at 24. He attended Hudson River Institute in New York, where he was taught history by John B. Van Petten, who had been an officer in the Civil War. While attending Syracuse University he enjoyed catching for the varsity baseball team more than studying for his classes. He passed only one class during his first semester, which was English Literature. He got an A. He was mostly known for chasing girls, skipping classes and reading poetry. His classmates later wrote, "Only women and other hero worshippers ever really liked him". The only schooling he ever took seriously was his military training. In 1892, Stephen fell deeply in love with Lily Brandon Munroe, the young wife of a wealthy geologist, who was frequently away on business. They were both staying at the Lake Avenue Hotel, and spent the summer attending dances, and strolling on the beach. Stephen begged her to run away with him, but after much consideration, she refused. In November of 1896, he met Cora Taylor, an older women, who had literary inclinations of her own. She became his companion for the rest of his life. Although she called herself Cora Crane and was introduced by Stephen as his wife, there is no evidence of their marriage. At the age of 28, his money mostly gone, and suffering from serious attacks of tuberculosis, Cora took him to a health spa in Badenweiler, Germany, where he died on June 5, 1900.*

"Far better it is to dare mighty things, to win glorious triumphs even though checkered by failure, than to rank with those poor spirits who neither enjoy nor suffer much because they live in the gray twilight that knows neither victory nor defeat"
Theodore Roosevelt

Marbled Pumpkin Cheesecake

1 ¼ CUP GRAHAM CRACKER CRUMBS

2 TABLESPOONS GRANULATED SUGAR

¼ CUP BUTTER, MELTED

2 CUPS SEMISWEET CHOCOLATE MINI-MORSELS, DIVIDED

3 PACKAGES (8 OUNCES EACH) CREAM CHEESE, SOFTENED

1 CUP GRANULATED SUGAR

¼ CUP LIGHT BROWN SUGAR, PACKED

1 ¾ CUP SOLID PACK PUMPKIN (16 OUNCE CAN)

4 LARGE EGGS

½ CUP EVAPORATED MILK, UNDILUTED

¼ CUP CORNSTARCH

¾ TEASPOON CINNAMON

1/8 TEASPOON NUTMEG

Crust

IN MEDIUM BOWL, COMBINE THE GRAHAM CRACKER CRUMBS, 2 TABLESPOONS OF SUGAR AND THE BUTTER. PRESS ONTO THE BOTTOM OF THE GREASED 10-INCH SPRINGFORM PAN; SPRINKLE WITH ONE CUP OF CHOCOLATE MORSELS.

Cheesecake

IN SMALL, HEAVY SAUCEPAN OVER THE LOW HEAT, MELT THE REMAINING MORSELS, STIRRING CONSTANTLY UNTIL SMOOTH. IN LARGE MIXER BOWL, BEAT CREAM CHEESE, GRANULATED AND BROWN SUGAR. MIX IN PUMPKIN, EGGS AND EVAPORATED MILK. BEAT IN CORNSTARCH, CINNAMON AND NUTMEG.

REMOVE ONE CUP OF THE PUMPKIN BATTER; STIR INTO THE MELTED CHOCOLATE. POUR REMAINDER OF THE PUMPKIN BATTER INTO THE SPRINGFORM PAN. POUR CHOCOLATE MIXTURE OVER THE TOP; SWIRL WITH A KNIFE. BAKE IN A PREHEATED OVEN AT 325 DEGREES FOR 60 MINUTES, OR UNTIL THE EDGE OF THE FILLING IS SET. TURN THE OVEN OFF AND ALLOW CHEESECAKE TO STAND IN OVEN FOR 30 MORE MINUTES. REMOVE FROM THE OVEN AND COOL COMPLETELY. COVER; CHILL FOR SEVERAL HOURS BEFORE SERVING.

DAVID COPPERFIELD
by
Charles Dickens

"Annual income twenty pounds, annual expenditures nineteen and six, result happiness. Annual income twenty pounds, annual expenditure twenty pounds ought and six, result misery."

Discussion Questions

• *Who do you think hurt the most, David, or his mother, Clara, when Mr. Murdstone and his sister took control of their home and family?*

• *Discuss Steerforth's character and how he affected others, especially Em'ly. What can we learn from their experiences?*

• *When did you realize the true character of Uriah Heep?*

• *Who would you consider the most lovable character in the story?*

• *Discuss some of the differences between David and Dora's relationship, and David and Agnes' relationship?*

Interesting Facts

When Charles Dickens was born, his family was rather well off, but like Mr. Micawber, Charles' father was lousy at managing his finances. Charles' father was sent to debtor's prison in 1824 when Charles was about twelve years old. When his father was taken to prison, Charles was sent to work for a boot-blackening manufacturer. He worked ten hour days for nearly a year and felt abandoned by his family. In the preface of **David Copperfield***, published in 1840, Charles Dickens wrote, "Of all my books, I like this the best." Dickens wrote to a friend, "If I were to say half of what* **David Copperfield** *makes me feel, tonight how strangely, even to you, I should be turned inside out! I seem to be sending some part of myself into the shadowy world." Like many of Dickens' other books,* **David Copperfield** *was released in installments. Dickens' serializations were widely known for their green covers. Dickens influenced many other popular writers of his time, including William Makepeace Thackeray and Wilkie Collins.*
*More interesting facts on Charles Dickens can be found on pages 36, 44, and 112.

"To become a real boy you must prove yourself brave, truthful, and unselfish."

from Pinnochio

Fresh Apple Pie

Pie Crust
¼ cup water
1/2 cup butter flavored shortening
1/2 teaspoon salt
1 cup flour

Mix ingredients in order quickly until just blended. Do not overwork the dough; the less it is handled, the flakier it will be. Roll out dough on a floured surface. Divide dough in half for top and bottom of pie. Place dough in pie pan and poke bottom and sides generously with fork.

Filling
8-10 sliced apples, enough to fill pie shell
2/3 cup sugar (or more)
1 ½ tablespoon flour
¼ teaspoon salt
1 ½ teaspoon lemon juice
¼ teaspoon nutmeg
½ teaspoon cinnamon
butter or margarine

Slice apples thick or thin to preference. Combine all ingredients except apples and butter. (The amount of sugar depends on tartness of apples.) Place one half of the apples in pie shell and sprinkle with one half of the sugar mixture. Top with the rest of the apples, heaping them in the center. Sprinkle the rest of the sugar mixture on top. Dot the top with butter or margarine. Cover with top crust or lattice strips. Bake at 425 degrees for 45 minutes. After 10 minutes check the crust for browning, and cover with foil (shiny side out) to prevent it becoming too dark.

"Blessed is the season which engages the
whole world in a conspiracy of love."

Hamilton Wright Maby

December

CHRISTMAS STORIES

Nothing will help you catch the spirit of Christmas like this month's selections of inspiring stories. Few things have thrilled us more than discussing one of these stories amongst the sparkling lights of the tree and a pile of beautifully wrapped gifts. Can you guess what the wrapped gifts contain? Books, of course, for our annual Christmas Book Exchange. After drawing numbered papers out of a bowl, we take turns unwrapping, stealing and swapping the books. (For more details, see the Preface.) Some members are lucky enough to go home with a copy of the next book club selection, while others are elated to take home the book that they brought, having always wanted to buy it for themselves. We also take home the fulfillment of a whole year of knowledge gained, recipes shared and friendships strengthened. For us, December is not only the celebration of the anniversary of our own book club, but of what book club has given to us –
Good Books, Good Food, and especially Good Friends!

A CHRISTMAS CAROL
and
CHRISTMAS BOOKS
by
Charles Dickens

"I don't know what to do!" cried Scrooge, laughing and crying in the same breath; and making a perfect Laocoon of himself with his stockings. " I am as light as a feather, I am as happy as an angel, I am as merry as a schoolboy. I am as giddy as a drunken man. A merry Christmas to everybody! A happy New Year to all the world!"

Discussion Questions

• *Did you perceive any symbolism in the characters? If so which character and why?*

• *What social commentaries do you feel Dickens made in this story with respect to the rich and the poor, the spiritual and the non-believers, etc.*

• *How does this story define the concept of Christmas for you?*

• *How are the three spirits that visit Scrooge different from each other?*

• *What aspects of his life did Scrooge change at the end of the story? What did he discover that he had misjudged about his life?*

Interesting Facts

Charles Dickens published **A Christmas Carol** *in 1843. It has become Dickens' best-known title and solidified him as the most popular writer of his time. Despite the popularity of the story,* **A Christmas Carol** *was an economic disaster. It was not advertised well and the low sale price made it impossible to cover the high production costs. The public loved* **A Christmas Carol** *so much that it became tradition for Dickens to write annual stories for the Christmas season.* **The Chimes** *and* **The Cricket on the Hearth** *are the most recognizable of these stories. It has been said by many that Charles Dickens is one of the greatest writers to have ever lived. Dickens separated from his wife in 1858 after becoming involved with a young actress, Ellen Ternam. He lost many friends and admirers as a result. Charles Dickens died June 9, 1870 at the age of 58. He was said to have died of over exertion while doing a lecture tour of America, a place he did not especially favor.*
More interesting facts on Charles Dickens can be found on pages 36, 44, and 108.

"Joy is not in things; it is in us."
Richard Wagner

English Toffee

2½ CUPS SUGAR
I POUND BUTTER
½ CUP WATER
¼ CUP LIGHT CORN SYRUP
I CUP SLIVERED ALMONDS
PINCH OF SALT
I BAG CHOCOLATE CHIPS
I CUP CHOPPED WALNUTS

MELT BUTTER IN A HEAVY SAUCEPAN, THEN ADD THE REMAINING INGREDIENTS AND BRING TO A BOIL. BOIL FOR APPROXIMATELY 20 MINUTES, OR UNTIL THE CANDY BECOMES A DEEP CARAMEL COLOR (LIKE THE COLOR OF A BROWN PAPER BAG). YOU CAN ALSO WATCH FOR A LITTLE PUFF OF SMOKE. AS SOON AS YOU SEE IT, REMOVE THE PAN FROM THE HEAT. POUR CANDY ONTO A COOKIE SHEET. LET COOL FOR FIVE MINUTES, THEN POUR A BAG OF CHOCOLATE CHIPS OVER THE TOP OF THE CANDY. THE CHOCOLATE WILL MELT AFTER A FEW MINUTES AND YOU CAN EASILY SPREAD IT OVER THE TOP OF THE CANDY WITH A SPATULA. SPRINKLE WITH CHOPPED WALNUTS. ONE OTHER OPTION IS TO LET THE CANDY COOL COMPLETELY WITHOUT THE CHOCOLATE. AFTERWARD, BREAK THE CANDY UP INTO PIECES AND DIP EACH PIECE INTO THE CHOCOLATE; THEN ROLL IN THE WALNUTS.

Tending Roses
by
Lisa Wingate

"My roses grew wild and died as I busied myself with feeding and diapering, nursery rhymes and sickbeds. I missed those bright blooms that had been mine an felt it unfair that I must leave my hard work there to die. But I did not think of it overmuch. My mind and heart were occupied with the sorrows and joys of motherhood. The day came, it seemed in no time, when my children were grown and gone, and I again found time to tend the roses. I could labor over them from dawn until dusk with no children to feed, no husband needing meals, and few passersby on the old road. My flowers have come thick and full and beautiful again. From time to time, I see neighbor children come to pick them when I am silent in my house. I close my eyes and listen to their laughter, and think that the best times of my life, the times that passed by me the most quickly, were the times when the roses grew wild."

Discussion Questions

• *Do you think Grandma Rose purposely left the notes for Katie to find? If so, why do you think that she chose this approach?*

• *Which of the many "life lessons" that Katie learned during her stay with her grandmother could you most relate to? From which lessons could our society most benefit today?*

• *Explore the relationship between Grandma Rose and Dell. What was your favorite interaction between the two? Who helped who the most?*

• *What can be learned from the "Christmas dinners to feed the hungry" family experience?*

Interesting Facts

Lisa Wingate has always loved to write. Her older brother taught her how to read and write before she went to kindergarten. She wrote and illustrated her first book that year, at the age of five, and has never quit. She had a first grade teacher who recognized her talent and started reading Lisa's stories aloud to the class. She quickly discovered the joys of having an audience and dreamed of one day being published. She attended Oklahoma State University and received her Bachelor's Degree in Technical English. While attending OSU, she met and married her husband, Sam. She worked as a technical writer, and wrote several computer manuals. During that time she continued to write and to sell free lance projects. She published several fiction and non fiction titles, but fiction is her first love. Lisa has said: "People inspire me. God inspires me. Love inspires me. Life's everyday miracles inspire me. I think most of us are stronger than we know, capable of more than we have ever imagined. I like to write about people pushing aside life's confines and roadblocks and setting the spirit free. I like to write about people forgetting the destination and enjoying the journey." Her novel, **Tending Roses***, was inspired by her own grandmother who, like Grandma Rose, loved to garden, give advice and calm fussy babies. She too left notes of family memories that Lisa kept and tucked away safely in a drawer. Lisa remembers her grandmother by stating, "She could be a grand instigator one minute, and a good Samaritan the next, selfish with one hand and generous with the other. I always knew she loved me, even when she was threatening to withhold our $5 birthday checks if we did not write to her more often." Her grandmother passed away at the age of 95, after being afflicted for several years with Alzheimer's Disease. Four years later she came across her grandmother's notes while cleaning out a drawer, and the ideas for the book flowed so fast that her fingers could hardly keep up on the computer. Lisa lives on a small ranch in Texas. She states, "I am the mother of two young sons who keep me running and keep me laughing. I wanted girls, I got boys. I never dreamed that boys could be so wonderful. But that is another story."*

"The stars are God's dreams, thoughts remembered in the silence of the night."

Henry David Thoreau

Chocolate Trifle

I CHOCOLATE CAKE MIX
I LARGE INSTANT CHOCOLATE PUDDING
I CAN PIE FILLING (CHERRY, RASPBERRY OR STRAWBERRY)
I LARGE CONTAINER OF WHIPPED TOPPING

MIX THE CAKE BATTER ACCORDING TO THE DIRECTIONS ON THE BOX. GREASE A JELLY ROLL PAN AND ADD THE BATTER. BAKE AT 350 DEGREES FOR I5 MINUTES OR UNTIL DONE. WHEN IT IS COOL, CUT THE CAKE INTO SMALL BITE SIZE PIECES. MIX PUDDING ACCORDING TO THE DIRECTIONS ON THE PACKAGE. IN A GLASS BOWL OR TRIFLE DISH, LAYER THE ABOVE INGREDIENTS IN THIS MANNER:

½ THE CAKE PIECES
½ THE PUDDING
½ THE PIE FILLING
½ THE WHIPPED TOPPING
REPEAT UNTIL FINISHED

LITTLE WOMEN
by
Louisa May Alcott

"Merry Christmas, Marmee! Many of them! Thank you for our books; we read some, and mean to every day," they cried, in chorus. "Merry Christmas, little daughters! I'm glad you began at once and hope you will keep on. But I want to say one word before we sit down. Not far away from here lies a poor woman with a little newborn baby. Six children are huddled into one bed to keep from freezing, for they have no fire. There is nothing to eat over there; and the oldest boy came to tell me they were suffering hunger and cold. My girls, will you give them your breakfast as a Christmas present?" They were all unusually hungry, having waited nearly an hour, and for a minute no one spoke; only a minute for Jo exclaimed impetuously, "I'm so glad you came before we began!" "May I go and help carry the things to the poor little children?" asked Beth eagerly. "I shall take the cream and the muffins," added Amy, heroically giving up the articles she most liked. Meg was already covering the buckwheats, and piling the bread into one big plate. ... The girls had never been called angel children before and thought it very agreeable, especially Jo, who had been considered a "Sancho" ever since she was born. That was a very happy breakfast, though they didn't get any of it; and when they went away, leaving comfort behind, I think there were not in all the city four merrier people then the hungry little girls who gave away their breakfasts and contented themselves with bread and milk on Christmas morning."

Discussion Questions

* *Which sister could you most relate to: Meg, Jo, Beth or Amy?*

* *How did the March Women influence the Laurence men? What was Jo's influence on Laurie?*

* *What changes came over the girls during Beth's illness? Their mother's return? Their fathers return?*

* *Where you surprised by Jo and Amy's marriages?*

* *What can we "reap" about the important things in life from the families' "harvest time" festivities at the end of the book?*

Interesting Facts

*Louisa May Alcott was born on November 29, 1832 in Germantown, Pennsylvania. Louisa became involved in the Civil War as a nurse in a large Washington hospital. She sent home many letters to her family before contracting with typhoid fever and being sent home. She called the letters **Hospital Sketches,** and in 1863 they were published in the Boston Commonwealth and later as a book. A partner from Roberts Brothers, Tomas Niles, had taken notice of **Hospital Sketches.** In 1867, he asked Louisa to write a book for girls. She would have rather written a fairy tale book, claiming that she did not understand girls. Niles insisted on it, and Louisa began writing it because she needed the money. She drew upon her own experiences, patterning Jo after herself and Meg, Beth and Amy after her own three sisters. Laurie's character was based on a boy named Ladislas Wisinewshi, whom she met while traveling in Europe with an invalid friend. She was twelve years his senior. Ralph Waldo Emerson, Nathanial Hawthorne and Henry Thoreau were all close family friends. Louisa's father was also friends with Henry Wadsworth Longfellow. She credited Emerson and Theodore Parker for much of her education. Louisa passed away March 6, 1888, having never married. Many gentleman in their later years admitted to having fond feelings for Louisa in their youth. Cornelia Meigs won The Newberry Medal for her biography of Louisa May Alcott entitled **Invincible Louisa**.*

"A thing of beauty is a joy forever. Its loveliness increases; it will never pass into nothingness."

John Keats

Peanut Butter Kiss Cookies

1 CUP BUTTER

1 CUP SUGAR

1 CUP BROWN SUGAR

2 EGGS

1 CUP CREAMY PEANUT BUTTER

1 TEASPOON VANILLA

CREAM THE ABOVE INGREDIENTS TOGETHER IN THE ORDER SHOWN ABOVE. NEXT ADD:

3 CUPS FLOUR

1 TEASPOON BAKING SODA

1 TEASPOON SALT

MIX IN THE REMAINING INGREDIENTS. SHAPE THE DOUGH INTO SMALL BALLS, AND ROLL THEM IN THE WHITE SUGAR. PLACE ON A GREASED COOKIE SHEET AND BAKE AT 375 DEGREES FOR 9-10 MINUTES.

16 OUNCE PACKAGE OF HERSHEY'S KISSES (UNWRAPPED)

WHEN COOKIES ARE DONE LET THEM COOL FOR 1-2 MINUTES, REMOVE FROM THE PAN AND PLACE A CHOCOLATE KISS ON TOP OF EACH COOKIE, PRESSING DOWN UNTIL THE SUGAR ON THE COOKIE CRACKS. ALLOW A COUPLE OF HOURS FOR THE KISSES TO COOL AND SET UP AGAIN BEFORE SERVING.

The Giver
by
Lois Lowry

"The man sighed, seeming to put his thought in order. Then he spoke again. 'Simply stated,' he said, 'although it's not really simple at all, my job is to transmit to you all the memories I have within me. Memories of the past.' He leaned back, resting his head against the back of the upholstered chair. 'It's the memories of the whole world,' he said with a sigh. 'Before you, before me, before the previous Receiver, and generations before him.' Jonas frowned. 'The whole world?' he asked him. The old man nodded to him. He looked drained, and a little sad. 'Sir?' Jonas said shyly. 'Yes. Do you have a question?' 'It's just that I don't know your name. I thought you were The Receiver, but you say that now I'm The Receiver. So I don't know what to call you.' The man had sat back down in the comfortable upholstered chair. He moved his shoulders around as if to ease away an aching sensation. He seemed terribly weary. 'Call me The Giver,' he told Jonas."

Discussion Questions

- *What elements in the society where Jonas grew up do you see in the world around you?*

- *At what point in the story did you realize the meaning of the term "released"?*

- *After completing the book, what were your thoughts and feeling about Jonas' parents?*

- *What do you think would be the most difficult job in the community?*

- *What do you think happened to the characters at the end of the book?*

Interesting Facts

Lois Lowry was on born March 20, 1937 in Honolulu, Hawaii to Robert and Katherine Hammersberg. Her father was a career Army officer and they lived at Schofield Barracks near Pearl Harbor. Lois was five years old when the attack on Pearl Harbor took place. Lois was sent to live with her maternal grandparents in the Amish Country of Pennsylvania. Her grandmother did not care much for children, but her grandfather adored her, and his comforting love protected her during the trauma of war. She attended school at Brown University and obtained her Associate's Degree in 1956. Later that year she married Donald Grey Lowry, an attorney, and together they had four children: Alix, Grey, Kristin and Benjamin.

*Once her children were all in school, she went back to school and in 1972 graduated with her Bachelor's Degree at the University of Southern Maine. She has also completed some graduate work. Lois has written numerous children's books. Her book, **Anastasia Krupnik**, was very successful and prompted her to write an entire series about the diminutive young heroine. Of Anastasia, Lowry writes, "I have the feeling she's going to go on forever – or until I get sick of her, which hasn't happened yet. I'm still very fond of her and her whole family." In 1990, Lowry received the Newberry Medal for her distinguished contribution to children's literature with **Number the Stars**. She also received the prestigious Newberry Medal a second time for **The Giver** in 1993. This book was a radical change from her previous works. When asked about the book's final chapter, Lowry states, "there is no single 'right' ending to the novel. There's a right one for each of us, and it depends on our own beliefs, on our own hopes . . . . Most of the young readers who have written to me have perceived the magic of the circular journey." Lowry has found success by translating her life into fiction for the purpose of helping others who may have suffered under similar circumstances. She also gauges her success as a writer by her ability to "help adolescents answer their own questions about life, identity and human relationships."*

"The birds of paradise alight only upon the hand that does not grasp."

John Berry

Chocolate Covered Caramel Pretzels

1 BAG PRETZEL RODS
1 POUND NESTLES CARAMEL
1 POUND WHITE CHOCOLATE
MILK CHOCOLATE
CHOPPED NUTS
SPRINKLES

CUT UP THE CARAMEL INTO AS MANY SQUARES AS YOU HAVE PRETZEL RODS. ROLL CARAMEL SQUARES BETWEEN YOUR HANDS TO FORM A SNAKE. TWIST CARAMEL DOWN THE PRETZEL ROD, LEAVING ONE INCH AT THE BOTTOM OF THE PRETZEL ROD TO HOLD. PUT WHITE CHOCOLATE IN A BOWL AND MICROWAVE FOR ONE MINUTE, REMOVE AND STIR. RETURN TO MICROWAVE FOR ANOTHER MINUTE, AND THEN STIR AGAIN. CONTINUE UNTIL THE CHOCOLATE IS COMPLETELY MELTED. POUR INTO A DRINKING GLASS. DIP THE CARAMEL COVERED PRETZELS INTO THE WHITE CHOCOLATE WHERE THE CARAMEL ENDS. LET THE EXCESS DRIP OFF, AND THEN PLACE ON A SHEET OF WAXED PAPER TO COOL. (WHEN DOING A LARGE QUANTITY, WRAP A HEATING PAD AROUND THE GLASS TO KEEP THE CHOCOLATE MELTED. THE CHOCOLATE COOLS QUICKLY AND HARDENS.) MELT MILK CHOCOLATE IN THE SAME MANNER AS THE WHITE CHOCOLATE. EITHER PLACE MILK CHOCOLATE IN A PASTRY BAG, OR DRIZZLE OFF THE END OF A SPOON, TO MAKE A ZIG-ZAG DESIGN ON THE THE PRETZEL. YOU MAY ALSO ROLL THE PRETZEL IN CHOPPED NUTS OR SPRINKLES.

Note: Nestle caramel and Guittard white chocolate is great for this recipe, but can only be found at specialty cake and candy stores. You can use caramel apple wraps that are available at most grocery stores if you can't locate the Nestle's, or visit the these websites: shepherdscakeandcandy.com or bakerscandc.com.

Main Gallery Entrance
Opening
Summer 2001